The Crown Glass Cutter and Glazier'S Manual

William Cooper

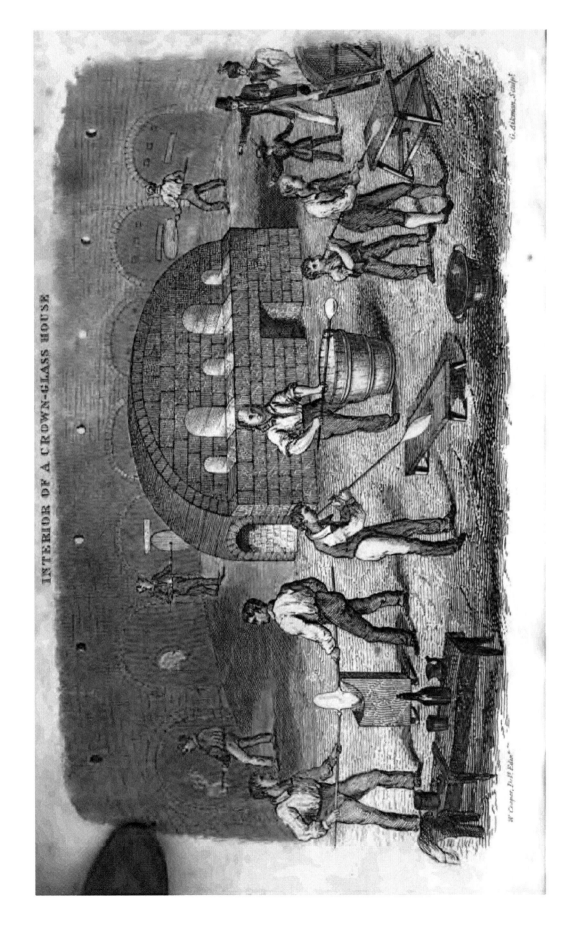

INTERIOR OF A CROWN-GLASS HOUSE

W.Cooper, Delt Edin.

G.Aikman Sculpt.

Crown Glass Cutter & Glaziers

MANUAL

BY WILLIAM COOPER

Glass Cutter, Glazier & Stained Glass maker in ordinary to the

KING for SCOTLAND

VIEW OF A CROWN GLASS HOUSE.

THE

CROWN GLASS CUTTER

AND

GLAZIER'S MANUAL.

BY

WILLIAM COOPER,

GLASS CUTTER, GLAZIER, AND STAINED GLASS-MAKER IN ORDINARY
TO THE KING FOR SCOTLAND.

ILLUSTRATED BY TWENTY-ONE ENGRAVINGS.

EDINBURGH:
OLIVER & BOYD; AND
SIMPKIN, MARSHALL, & CO. LONDON.
1835.

221.

[ENTERED AT STATIONERS' HALL.]

EDINBURGH:
Printed by Andrew Shortrede, Thistle Lane.

CONTENTS.

PLATES.

PREFACE.

———

THE general diffusion of knowledge, and the improvements in the modes of its dissemination which have occurred within these few years, have made literature as familiar in the workshop of the artisan as in the closet of the student. There has thus been opened up to the labouring part of the community one of the purest sources of enjoyment, and the means suggested to the enterprising mechanic, whereby he may greatly extend the sphere of his own usefulness. It has likewise not unfrequently inspired him with a laudable ambition to contribute his quota to the general stock of knowledge through the medium of the press — to employ his pen as well as the implements of his trade — to teach as well as to practise.

This association of literature with mechanical skill must have a beneficial effect in two respects. In

the first place, its tendency is to raise the humblest
mechanical trades to the rank of sciences, and im-
part to the workman a sense of the worth and
importance of his art, and such a knowledge, as
well of its theory as its practice, as every craftsman
ought to possess. It will elevate his own character
by elevating that of his art, and, while it promotes
his general intellectual advancement, it will, in the
second place, enable him to refine and improve on
that art to an extent which must soon be felt in
the comforts, elegancies, and conveniencies of life.
We cannot but think that the skill and ingenuity of
the mechanic, in ordinary things, are not sufficiently
prized, and this merely because, from not being
sufficiently known, they are accounted ordinary
things. We look with indifference on the produce
of his intellect and the works of his hands, and say,
with an emphasis which is meant to deprive him of
all merit, " It is his trade." True, it may be his
trade, but what of that? Has there been no mind
at work to regulate, no genius to direct his manual
dexterity? Yes; in the meanest mechanical art
there is much of these qualities displayed. Genius
has, indeed, been allowed to the tradesman, and this
quality of mind has been denominated mechanical
genius. Now, whilst this term is understood merely

in a discriminative sense, to distinguish it from the other forms under which genius appears, and when it is not associated with any ideas of inferiority, it is well enough; but when it is understood as coupled with certain ideas of inferiority, we cannot assent to the propriety of that disparagement of the faculty which is thus implied; for it cannot be denied, that genius exercised in making a shoe, or in any other piece of workmanship, is as distinctly and purely genius as that faculty developed in writing a book. It is true, that in the former of these works it appears in a less dignified form than in the latter, but is its result less an emanation of genius on that account? A diamond is a diamond still, whether it be placed on the blue bonnet of the peasant, or the monarch's crown; and who knows but that the genius which may have discovered itself in the humble and homely form spoken of, might have raised its possessor to a high place amongst men, had his destiny been otherwise ordered? Or who can say, that what is called mechanical genius, may not often be an accident of the quality, the result of a chance direction of its powers; thus making it possible, that Watt and Bonaparte might have exchanged places, without loss of any of that fame, which we now associate with the names of these

b

extraordinary men. Apart from these considerations, however, who does not see, that the discoveries of Watt have been infinitely more valuable to mankind, and are attended with a much purer glory, than the matchless but desolating conquests of Bonaparte ?

Leaving these speculations, we proceed to speak of the little work which these preliminary observations are meant to introduce to the reader. Some of the reasons which dictated its publication have been already alluded to, but there are others which have been still more influential than any of these.

It may be held as a maxim, it is presumed, that every man desirous of advancing to excellence in his business, should know something of its past history, its present circumstances, and its future prospects ; and it was under this impression, combined with the idea that he could communicate some useful information to the glazier, that the writer threw together, into the shape in which he now presents it, the result of some experience in his trade, and some reading on the subject of the article in which he deals.

As the title of the work implies, it has been written chiefly with a view to explain and illustrate the art of glazing. In those parts of it, therefore, which do not bear directly upon this subject, only general information has been communicated. Upon glass cutting, however, several hints and observations have been given, which, it is hoped, will be found serviceable to the crown glass-cutter and glazier. In the historical department, and process of manufacturing, such information has been given, as every glazier, it is conceived, ought to possess.* The writer makes no pretension whatever to the merit of suggesting any thing new, or of adding to the general stock either of chemical or scientific knowledge. In the article on staining and stained glass, though forming a part of the writer's own business, it has not been thought proper to give more than a general outline, because it was believed, that the numbers interested in it as a trade were too few to warrant his entering into details on the subject, in a work intended principally, as already said, for the glazier, to whom these could only be of secondary interest.

Tables for the measurement of glass might themselves form a volume. All the calculations necessary for ordinary purposes are given in four pages.

* For a more detailed account of the history and manufacture of glass in all its branches, see article Glass, in the new edition of the *Encyclopedia Britannica*, by the same writer.

In large quantities, the glazier would do well to
go through the calculations himself, according to
the plan laid down, which a little practice will
enable him to do with ease.

EDINBURGH, *January*, 1835.

HISTORY OF GLASS.

CHAPTER I.

INTRODUCTORY.

THE word *Glass* has been variously derived, but is still of uncertain origin. The reader may take his choice of the two derivations usually given, and which, of all the others, appear to be the most plausible, namely, *glassum*, the name given to amber by the ancient Gauls, and *glacies*, the Latin name of ice.

The first discovery of the art of manufacturing glass is of such remote antiquity, as to be altogether beyond the reach of inquiry. It precedes the commencement of history, and is connected with its earliest records, by a tradition which is again lost in the obscurity of time. Glass beads, and other ornaments made of that substance, skilfully manufactured, and beautifully coloured, have been found adorning the bodies of Egyptian mummies,

A

which have been ascertained to be upwards of
three thousand years old. There are, besides these
ancient relics, many other proofs of this art having
long preceded the Christian era.

Glass is distinctly mentioned in the book of Job,
and is also spoken of by Aristophanes, in his
comedy of the *Clouds*, four hundred and twenty-
three years before the birth of Christ.

Pliny, the Roman historian, gives a sufficiently
plausible account of the first discovery of the art of
manufacturing this beautiful and useful commodity,
but it has all the appearance of being merely an
ingenious fable; well enough conceived, but
undeserving of much credit. He says, that a ship
laden with fossil alkali, a component part of glass,
having been driven ashore on the coast of Palestine,
the sailors accidentally placed their cooking vessels
on pieces of the alkali. The river sand on which
the operation of preparing their food was performed,
being vitrified by its union with the alkali, through
the agency of the fire which they used, produced
glass; and hence, according to Pliny, the discovery
of the art.

The story bears evident marks of having been
got up, *a posteriori*, to suit the circumstances of the
case, and its artificial adaptation to this purpose is

so palpable, as to destroy all faith in its credibility. There are, besides, many simple processes by which the art of glass-making might be discovered, such as the burning of bricks, which, after undergoing this operation, are more or less vitrified, or covered with an imperfect glass; and, indeed, it has been asserted, that the idea of glass-making originated from this very circumstance.

Whenever, or by whatever means, the art of glass-making was first invented, it is certain that it is of the highest antiquity—of an antiquity so remote, indeed, that it has hitherto defied all research; and this should be nearly enough to satisfy any reasonable curiosity on the subject.

Although there is much uncertainty regarding the period when this art was first discovered, there is none as to the quarter of the world in which that discovery took place. This was the East, the original seat of nearly all the arts and sciences. Though first discovered there, however, and practised from time immemorial, the art of glass-making was confined for many centuries to the production merely of ornaments, no idea having ever occurred that it might be extended to the manufacture of really useful articles, such as domestic vessels, windows, or mirrors.

The first glass-houses mentioned in history, were erected in Tyre, an ancient Phœnician city, on the coast of Syria. The towns of Sidon and Alexandria, also, belonging to the same people, became afterwards celebrated for the manufacture of this article. To these places the art was exclusively confined for many centuries, and during this time they alone supplied the world with its produce.

From the circumstance of coloured glass beads and amulets having been found in Druidical remains in this country, it has been asserted that the art of making glass was known in Britain before the invasion of the Romans; but this is wholly incredible. It cannot be believed, that a people, who were in a state little, if at all, removed from primitive barbarity, and who, it is known, were entirely unacquainted with any other art, should be found not only versant in the manufacture of glass, a complicated and highly ingenious process, but should excel in it; for the beads and amulets spoken of are of exquisite workmanship, and beautifully coloured in imitation of the rarest and most precious stones. There seems little doubt, therefore, that the ancient Britons procured these in traffic with the Tyrians, who would visit the island as we do those in the South Seas, to drive a trade with its savage inhabitants in toys and trinkets, giving them these in exchange for skins, or other natural productions. By whatever means, however, these ornaments found their way into Britain, it is certain' that they were in extensive use, though principally for religious purposes, long prior to the Roman invasion, as they are found in barrows and tumuli of a much older date than that period: one of the former, in particular, at Stonehenge, on being opened, was found filled with them. Another remarkable proof of the high antiquity of the art of glass making, and of the early perfection of which it boasts, is exhibited in a large plate of glass which was found in Herculaneum, an ancient city in Italy, which was destroyed by an eruption of Vesuvius in the year of our Lord 79.

From Syria, where, as already mentioned, the manufacture of glass was first established on an extensive scale, or something like system, it gradually travelled west: the Greeks acquired it, and from thence it found its way to Rome; but its march was slow, and for many centuries the Romans were supplied from Alexandria.

The shape in which it was imported thither, however, still bespoke a limited knowledge of its uses. That shape was principally ornamental,— occasionally, and in rare cases, it extended to drinking cups, or glasses, but these were deemed fit only for a king; and though an excellence in colouring glass was attained at this early period, and long before, which is not yet surpassed, the art of producing it free from any colour — the most difficult part of the process of glass-making, since it is readily affected by extraneous substances — was scarcely known; for we are told that the emperor Nero paid six thousand sestertia * for two drinking cups, whose value chiefly arose from the circumstance of their being entirely colourless. The poorest and meanest persons of the present day drink out of glasses in which this property is perfect.

The glass ware imported into Rome from Alexandria, was, as already noticed, principally ornamental, and all coloured; but this colouring was so exquisite, and the workmanship otherwise of these little fragile toys so beautiful, that they were used and valued as jewels, and so employed in adorning the persons of the ancient Roman belles and beaux; and thus a string of glass beads, which no servant girl would now wear, was considered an ornament to which the daughter of a patrician only could pretend.

* A sum nearly equal to £50,000 sterling.

The art of making for themselves that article for which they had hitherto been indebted to the Tyrians, at length found its way to Rome. In the reign of the emperor Tiberius, a company of glass manufacturers established themselves in the city, and had a street assigned them in its first region; but the produce of their manufacture was very early considered a fit subject of taxation, an impost having been laid upon it by Alexander Severus, in the year 220.

Pliny, of whose credibility we have already spoken, relates that a glass-maker, who had invented a species of malleable glass, brought a vessel made of that material to Tiberius. To shew the emperor the singular property of his glass, he dashed the vessel on the floor with sufficient force to dimple it, and impair its shape. He then took a hammer, and, in the presence of the emperor, hammered it into its original form, removing the dimples, and restoring the beauty of its shape. Instead of rewarding the ingenious artist for this proof of his extraordinary skill, Tiberius ordered him to be instantly beheaded —alleging that this discovery, if known, would render gold and silver useless. Such is the story of Pliny, but like many of his other stories, it deserves no credit.

The precise period at which the Romans extended their knowledge of the art of glass-making to window glass, and when they first used it for the purposes for which it is now employed in that form, is not certainly known. Previous to such application of the art, at whatever time it may have first taken place, the Roman windows were filled with a semi-transparent substance called *lapis specularis*, a fossil of the class of *talcs*, which readily splits into thin, smooth laminæ, or plates. This substance is found in masses of about ten or twelve inches in breadth, and three in thickness; and when sliced, very much resembles horn, for which it is to this day often employed by lantern makers. The Romans were chiefly supplied with this article from the island of Cyprus, where it abounds; and so good a substitute is it said to have been for glass, that besides being applied to the purpose of admitting light into the Roman houses, it was also used by them in the construction of hot-houses, for raising and protecting delicate plants from the inclemency of the weather; and by being so employed, we are told that the emperor Tiberius had cucumbers at his table throughout the whole year.

Although the precise period of the introduction of glass into windows is not known, it is yet certain that it was applied to this purpose as early as the year 422; for glass windows are distinctly mentioned by St Jerome, who flourished about that period. They are again spoken of, and represented as being fastened in with plaster, by Johannes Philippinus, who lived in 630.

Bede asserts, that glass windows were first introduced into England in the year 674, by Abbot Benedict, who brought over artificers skilled in the art of making window-glass, to glaze the church and monastery of Weremouth.

Another authority attributes the introduction of this luxury to Bishop Wilfred, junior, who died in 711. As the periods mentioned by these authorities do not differ very widely, it seems probable that glass windows were first introduced into England either about the end of the seventh or the beginning of the eighth century. The use of window glass, however, was then, and for many centuries after, confined entirely to buildings appropriated to religious purposes; but, in the fourteenth century, it was so much in demand, though still confined to sacred edifices and ornamental purposes, that glazing had become a regular trade. This appears from a contract entered into by the church authorities of York Cathedral, in 1338, with a glazier to glaze the west windows of that structure, a piece of work which he undertook to perform at the rate of sixpence per foot for white glass, and one shilling per foot for coloured. Glass windows, however, did not become common in England till the close of the twelfth century.

Until this period they were rarely to be found in private houses, and were deemed a high refinement in luxury, and a mark of great magnificence. Previous to this era, the windows of houses in Britain were filled with prepared oiled paper, or wooden lattices; and in cathedrals, the latter and sheets of linen supplied the place of glass till the eighth century. In meaner edifices, lattices continued in use till the eighteenth. These were fixed in frames of wood, called capsamenta, from which is derived the word casement, now applied to the framework of a window.

We are told that the manufacturing of window glass was first introduced into England in 1557. But it is evident, from a contract, spoken of by Horace Walpole, in his *Anecdotes of Painting*, between the Countess of Warwick and John Prudde of Westminster, glazier, whom she employed, with other tradesmen, to erect and embellish a magnificent tomb for the earl her husband, that window glass was made in England upwards of a century before that period. In this curious treaty, which is dated 1439, John Prudde is bound to use " no glass of England, but glass from beyond the seas." But it will be observed that the document, besides shewing that the art of making window glass was known and practised in England in the fifteenth century, seems also to shew that it was of inferior quality to that which could be obtained from abroad.

The art of manufacturing glass, which we have traced from the Egyptians, as exhibited in the decorations of their mummies, to the Phœnicians, and from them to the Romans, lingered long in Italy, where it was brought to a degree of perfection wholly unknown before. Some beautiful specimens of this proficiency of the Roman people in the art are found in ancient tumuli, the sepultures of their dead. These are bottles or vessels called lachrymatories, typically represented as containing the tears which were shed for the deceased by his or her surviving and sorrowing friends. These have been found of various shapes and sizes, but all exhibiting great excellence of workmanship.

The seat of the art, however, in process of time, changed from Rome to Venice, or rather to Murano, a little village in the neighbourhood of that city, where extensive works were established; but the produce was always recognized by the name of Venetian glass. We are told by Baron Von Lowhen, in his *Analysis of Nobility in its Origin*, that " So useful were the glass-makers at one period at Venice, and so considerable the revenue accruing to the republic from their manufacture, that, to encourage the men engaged in it to remain in Murano, the senate made them all burgesses of Venice, and allowed nobles to marry their daughters; whereas, if a nobleman marries the daughter of any other tradesman, the issue were not reputed noble."

For many years this glass surpassed any that was made elsewhere, and commanded nearly the whole sale of Europe.

The ingenuity of the Venetians in glass-making was especially remarkable in the great improvement which they made in the manufacture of mirrors. This new application of glass was first attempted at Sidon, about the thirteenth century; previous to which period, polished plates of metal were used at the toilette, and, in the rudeness of the first ideas which suggested the substitution of glass, the latter was made of a deep black colour to imitate them. This opacity was farther increased by laying black foil behind them. Thus it was thought that the nearer they could be brought to resemble plates of dark metal, the nearer they approached perfection.

The metal mirrors, however, notwithstanding this attempt to imitate them, kept their hold long after the introduction of their fragile rivals; but the latter finally triumphed, and the metallic mirrors at length wholly disappeared,—a result accomplished chiefly by the skill of the Venetians, who effected such improvements in their manufacture, that they speedily acquired a celebrity which secured an immense sale for them throughout Europe and the Indies. Glass mirrors came into general use about the fourteenth century.

From Venice, the art of glass-making found its way into France, where an attempt was made, in 1634, to rival the Venetians in the manufacture of mirrors. The first essay was unsuccessful, but another made in 1665, in which Venetian workmen were employed, had better fortune, though, in a few years afterwards, this establishment, which was situated in the village of Tourlaville, near Cherbourg, in Lower Normandy, was also threatened with ruin by a discovery, or rather improvement in the art of glass-making, effected by one Abraham Theverat. This improvement consisted in casting plates of much larger dimensions than had been hitherto thought practicable. Theverat cast his first plates at Paris, and astonished every artist by their magnitude. These plates were eighty-four inches in height and fifty in breadth, while none before had ever exceeded forty-five or fifty inches in length. Theverat was bound by his patent to make all his plates at least sixty inches in length and forty in breadth. The two companies, Theverat's and that at Tourlaville, united their interest, but were so unsuccessful that, in 1701, they were unable to pay their debts, and were, in consequence, compelled to abandon several of their furnaces. In 1702 a new company was formed, under the management of Antoine d'Agincourt, which realized handsome profits to its proprietors, a circumstance which is attributed wholly to the greater prudence of D' Agincourt.

We are told that, early in the fourteenth century, the French government made a concession in favour of glass-making, decreeing not only that no derogation from nobility should follow the practice of the art, but that none, save gentlemen, or the sons of noblemen, should venture to engage in any of its branches, even as working artisans.

This restriction was accompanied by the grant of

a royal charter of incorporation, conveying various important privileges, under which the occupation became eventually a source of great wealth to several families of distinction, whose descendants have, at different times, attained some of the highest dignities of the state.

The exact period when the art of manufacturing glass was first introduced into England is not easily determined. As already mentioned, it is said to have been brought to this country in 1557; but we have stated a circumstance which, we conceive, leaves little doubt that glass was manufactured there at a much earlier date. In 1557, however, it certainly was manufactured in England. The finer sort of window glass was then made at Crutched Friars, in London.

The first flint-glass made in England was manufactured at Savoy House in the Strand, and the first plate-glass, for looking-glasses, coach-windows, &c. was made at Lambeth, in 1673, by Venetian workmen brought over by the Duke of Buckingham.

The date of the introduction of the art of glass-making into Scotland is more easily determined, because of more recent occurrence. It took place in the reign of James VI. An exclusive right to manufacture glass within the kingdom for the space of thirty-one years, was granted by that monarch to Lord George Hay in the year 1610. This right his Lordship transferred, 1627, for a considerable sum, to Thomas Robinson, merchant tailor in London, who again disposed of it for £250, to Sir Robert Mansell, vice-admiral of England. The first manufactory of glass in Scotland, an extremely rude one, was established at Wemyss in Fife. Regular works were afterwards erected at Prestonpans, and at Leith.*

Crown-glass is now manufactured at Warrington, St Helens, Eccleston, Old Swan, and Newton, Lancashire; at Birmingham, Hunslet near Leeds, and Bristol. It is also manufactured of excellent quality on the Tyne and Wear.† Great improve-

---

* A bottle was blown at the Leith glass works, January 7, 1747–8, of the extraordinary capacity of one hundred and five imperial gallons. A neat pocket pistol for the moors !

† A very extensive crown-glass manufactory in the west of Scotland has, on account of the lamented death of some of the principals, been lately struck from the list of working establishments. A good many years since, one of the partners of this house, in a spirit somewhat similar to that which induced Peter the Great of Russia to leave his state at home and come to England to work as a common carpenter in the naval dock-yards of that kingdom, went to, and wrought as an ordinary journeyman glass-blower in several crown-glass houses in England. The result of

ments have recently been made in the manufacture of crown-glass; and we believe this article, as now manufactured in England, is superior in point of quality to that of any other nation.

With regard to the art of staining or painting glass, (an art so blended with the history of the substance itself, that some notice of it becomes indispensable in a sketch of this description,) there is good reason to believe that it is coeval with the art of making glass, since, as has been noticed in another part of this sketch, it is a matter of difficulty to make it without colour. Thus the possibility of subjecting this propensity to the will of the manufacturer must have very easily occurred, although it certainly requires both much art and chemical knowledge to produce perfect specimens of this description of manufacture; yet this perfection, including, of course, all the necessary art and chemical knowledge, seems to have been attained at a period as remote as tradition itself. The tradition relating to this subject bears, that the art of tinging glass was the invention of an Egyptian king; but

this determined and extraordinary zeal was, that the house in which the gentleman alluded to was interested became unrivalled for the excellence of its crown-glass. The fame of its manufacture spread far and wide, and its prosperity was proportioned to its reputation.

B

whether it was so or not, it is certain that the art has been known in Egypt for many thousand years, and the most beautiful imitations of precious stones, blue, green, crimson, &c. of this date are still extant. That the colouring of glass, even when in the shape of domestic vessels, is of high antiquity, appears from the circumstance of the Emperor Adrian having received as a present from an Egyptian priest, two glass cups which sparkled with colours of every kind, and which he prized so highly for their singular beauty and magnificence, that he ordered that they should be produced only on great occasions. The art, however, of combining the various colours so as to produce pictures, is of more recent origin. The earlier specimens of this branch of the art discover a factitious joining of different pieces of glass, differently tinged, and so arranged as to produce the figure, or figures, wanted, and are thus little else than a sort of mosaic work. The various pieces are held together generally by a vein of lead, run upon the back of the picture, precisely at their junction.

Modern ingenuity has superseded this clumsy expedient, and every colour used in painting can now be introduced into one entire sheet. It is asserted that, for a long period, the pictured glass which was used in cathedrals, &c. was merely painted on the surface—the art of incorporating the colours with the glass by fusion, the method now practised, being unknown till about the close of the fifteenth century.

This great and singular improvement is ascribed to a painter of Marseilles, who went to Rome during the pontificate of Julius II; but his discovery went no farther than that of producing different colours on different pieces of glass, and having them afterwards united in the manner spoken of above. This art was, at a later period, greatly improved by Albert Durer, and Lucas of Leyden, the latter of whom brought it nearly to perfection.

The first painted glass done in England was in the time of King John : previous to this, all stained or painted glass was imported from Italy.   The next notice of it occurs in the reign of Henry III. The treasurer of that monarch orders that there be painted, on three glass windows in the chapel of St John, a little Virgin Mary holding the child, and the Trinity, and Saint John the Apostle. At an after period, he issues another mandate for two painted windows in the hall.

Even at this early period, however, England boasted of eminent native artists in glass painting, amongst the first of whom was John Thornton, glazier of Coventry. This person was employed, in the time of Henry IV, by the Dean and Chapter of York Cathedral, to paint the east window of that splendid edifice; and for the beautiful and masterly workmanship which he exhibited in this specimen of his skill, he received four shillings per week of regular wages. He was bound to finish the work in less than three years, and to receive, over and above the weekly allowance, one hundred shillings for each year; and if the work was done to the satisfaction of his employers, he was to receive, on its completion, a farther gratuity of Ten Pounds.

From this period, downwards, there have been many skilful native artists, although the Reformation greatly impeded the progress of the art, by banishing the ungodly ostentation of ornamented windows from churches: indeed, so serious was this interruption, that the art had nearly altogether disappeared in the time of Elizabeth. Amongst the most eminent glass painters who first appeared on the revival of the art after this period, were Isaac Oliver, born in 1616, and one William Price, who lived about the close of the seventeenth century. This last person was the only glass painter in England for many years. He is said to have discovered, what has ever since been a desideratum in the art of glass staining, the secret of producing a rich, clear, bright, and transparent red, the most difficult to strike, and the most expensive of all the colours employed in glass painting.

Price having died soon after making this discovery, it is said to have died with him. This artist was succeeded by a person at Birmingham, who, in 1757, fitted up a window for Lord Lyttleton in the Church of Hajely. This glass painter was again succeeded by one Peckite, at York, who attained considerable eminence in the art.

During all this time, however, and, indeed, up to a comparatively recent date, painted glass was considered as too costly and too magnificent an article to be otherwise employed than in decorating religious edifices, or the palaces of nobles; and even in the latter case it was but sparingly used.

Modern improvement has now placed this beautiful ornament within the reach of very ordinary circumstances, and when this is considered, it must excite a strong feeling of surprise to find how little so elegant and refined a luxury is even yet in demand. On this subject we shall say more hereafter under its proper head.

The consequence of this rarity of painted glass was, that even so lately as 1753 it was considered

in the light of a curiosity, and never dreamt of as
an article which might come into common use for
domestic purposes.   In the year just mentioned, an
Italian, named Asciotti, brought over a parcel of
painted glass from Flanders, which he sold at a
good price in London.   Encouraged by his success,
his wife and himself made a regular trade of import-
ing the article, and paid stated periodical visits to
the Continent for the purpose of procuring fresh
parcels.   These were mostly bought up by one
Palmer, a glazier, who raised the price from one
and two to five guineas for a single piece—an
enormous increase upon his first charges; as Horace
Walpole, who gives this information, tells us that
he had bought from the same man four hundred
and fifty pieces, for which he paid only thirty-six
guineas, and this specifically included the expense
of Asciotti's journey.

Eight years after this, namely, 1761, one Paterson,
an auctioneer in the Strand, had a public sale of
painted glass, the first time that this article ever
appeared in England in such circumstances.

CHAPTER II.

PROCESS OF MANUFACTURING.

THERE are various species of glass, each produced by a different process of manufacture, and composed of different materials, and of different proportions of the same material; but, in a work of this nature, which is chiefly intended for the glass-cutter and glazier, it does not seem necessary to speak of any other description of it than that which their trade leads them almost exclusively to employ. We shall therefore confine ourselves to crown, or window-glass, employing as few technical phrases as possible.

Crown, or window-glass, is usually composed of only two materials,—these are kelp and fine white sand. The place of the former, however, is sometimes supplied by pearl ashes, or by some other alkalis, but of these we consider it foreign to our purpose to speak. Kelp is a substance produced by the burning of what is called, in the learned world, *fuci*, but which will be better and more generally understood by the familiar name of sea-weed, or wrack. Of this marine vegetable there are various kinds, all designated by different classical names, which we need not enumerate. These are cut from the rocks in the months of May, June, and July. After being so cut and brought to shore, the weed, or wrack, is spread out to dry, that it may burn the more readily, and is then thrown into a pit lined with stones, in which a large fire of peat has been previously kindled. On this fire the weed is heaped from time to time, until a large mass is accumulated, and the whole is reduced to a state of fusion. It is then well mixed and levelled, and allowed gradually to cool. When sufficiently cold, it is taken from the pit, and broken into portable masses for the convenience of transportation. With regard to the other component part of window-glass, namely, sand, the best description for the purposes of the glass-maker is procured from Lynn Regis in Norfolk. The superiority of this sand arises from the circumstance of its containing a greater quantity of minute transparent crystals than is found in the sand of any other place in this country.

When the two materials of which we have been speaking come into the possession of the glass-maker, for the purposes of his manufacture, they are thus treated, previously to their being employed in the formation of glass: The kelp is broken into small pieces, either by the hand or by a machine called a stamper. It is then put into a mill, ground to a fine powder, and afterwards passed through a brass-wire sieve.

Having undergone this operation, it is removed into the mixing room, the apartment where the proportions of material are adjusted, and where, as the name implies, they are mingled together previous to their being *fritted*, or calcined. The sand, again, is usually washed in a large vat with boiling or cold water, until the latter runs off quite clear. When not washed, the effect of this operation is produced by the use of nitre during the process of calcining, which consumes any sulphureous matter that may be present, or extraneous substances of an animal or vegetable nature, and reduces them to an earth not injurious to glass. The sand, it may be observed, is sometimes put into an annealing or calcining arch, where it is subjected to a strong heat for twenty-four hours, and kept during that time in a red-hot state, and then plunged into water. This operation has the effect of dividing the particles of sand, and making it unite more readily with the alkali during the process of calcining. When this operation is completed, the sand is also removed into the mixing room. Here the materials, the sand

and the kelp powder, are carefully proportioned, generally in the degree of one part of the former to two parts of the latter, and mingled together according to the judgment of the mixer, an operation which requires great care and experience. When thoroughly mixed, the compost is put into a calcining arch, or reverberatory furnace, where it is subjected to a heat so strong as to reduce it to a semi-fluid state. This substance, which is called *frit*, is now taken from the furnace, spread upon a plate of iron while yet hot, and afterwards, but before it becomes quite cool, divided into large cakes. The last operation consists in throwing the frit into the melting pot, which is of this form:

This pot is made of the finest clay. The best is got from Stourbridge, and goes through a tedious and exceedingly troublesome process of drying, annealing, or tempering, &c. before it is fit for its ultimate purpose. To the frit thrown into this pot there is added a proportion of cullet, or broken crown-glass. In about thirty to thirty-six hours, the whole is reduced, by a powerful heat, to fine liquid glass, and is then ready for the operations of the workman.

The furnace is then slackened, and the metal being now in a workable state, the first operator who approaches the furnace in which the pot of liquid glass is placed, is the "skimmer," who skims off, or removes all extraneous or crude substances from the surface of the metal. Next follows the "gatherer," who is provided with an iron pipe, or tube, about six or seven feet in length, and of this shape :

Having previously heated that end of the tube which comes in contact with the glass, he dips it into the pot of metal, and by turning it gently round, gathers about one and a half pounds of liquid glass on the end of it. Having allowed this to cool for a short time, he again dips it into the pot, and gathers an additional quantity, of from two and a half to three pounds. This is also permitted to cool as before, when the operation of dipping is again repeated, and a sufficient quantity of metal, about nine or ten pounds weight, is **gathered**, to form what is technically called a **table**, **or** sheet of glass about to be blown. The rod **thus** loaded is held for a few seconds in a perpendicular position, that the metal may distribute itself equally on all sides, and that it may, by its own **weight**, *be* lengthened out beyond the rod. The operator then moulds the metal into a regular form, by *rolling* it on a smooth iron plate called the "marver," a corruption of the French word *marbre*.

He then blows strongly through the tube, *when* his breath, penetrating the centre of the red-hot mass of glass, forms it into a hollow vessel of the shape of a pear, thus,—

The tube, with the elongated sphere of glass at the end of it, is then handed to the blower, who heats it once more, and again at the furnace; and alternately, or between each blowing, he presses the end against the bullion bar, so called from the part thus pressed forming the centre of the sheet, or bull's eye, thus,

By the dexterous management of this operation, the glass assumes somewhat of a spherical form.

The blower heats a third time at the bottoming hole, and blows the glass into a full sized globe, thus,—

Again applying it to the same furnace, the globe of glass, by the agency of the fire, assumes a circular form, as shewn in the following Figure.

When this part of the process has been completed, and the glass has been allowed to cool a little, it is rested on the casher box, and an iron rod, called a "pontil, or punty rod," on which a little hot metal has been previously gathered to make it adhere, is attached to the flattened side, exactly

opposite the hollow tube which is now detache
means of a piece of iron previously dipped in
water, leaving a circular hole in the glass of ɛ
two inches diameter. The following figure rɛ
sents the operation of attaching the punty.

Taking hold of the punty rod, the workman
presents the glass to another part of the fu
called the " nose hole," where, it must be obse
the aperture made by its separation from the tɩ
now presented, and at which it is kept until i
become sufficiently ductile to adapt it for the o
tion of the flashing furnace. Being here tɩ

dexterously round, slowly at first, and afterwards with greater rapidity, the glass yields to the centrifugal force, and thus necessarily enlarges the aperture above alluded to.

The workman, taking great care to preserve, by a regular motion, the circular figure of the glass, proceeds to whirl it round with increasing velocity, until the aperture, now diminished to a ring of only a few inches diameter, suddenly flies open with a loud ruffling noise, like the rapid unfurling of a flag in a strong wind, and leaves the glass a circular plane or sheet, of from four to four and a half feet diameter, of equal thickness throughout, except at the point called the bullion, or bull's eye, where it is attached to the iron rod. The following figure will give some idea of this very beautiful part of the process of glass making.

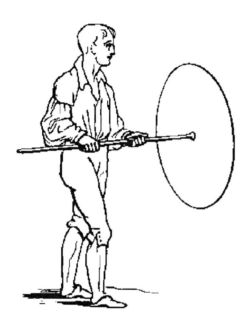

The sheet of glass, now fully expanded, is moved round with a moderate velocity, until it is sufficiently cool to retain its form. It is carried to the mouth of the kiln, or annealing arch, where it is rested on a bed of sand, and detached from the punty rod. The sheet or table is then lifted on a wide pronged fork, called a faucet, and put into the arch, where it is tempered by being subjected to a

gradually decreasing heat for about twenty-four hours. When taken from the arch at the end of this period, the glass, after an account has been taken of it by the exciseman, is ready for the glazier's use. It is first, however, removed to the manufacturer's warehouse, where the circular sheets are cut into halves, and assorted into the different qualities well known to the tradesman by the names of seconds, thirds, and fourths.

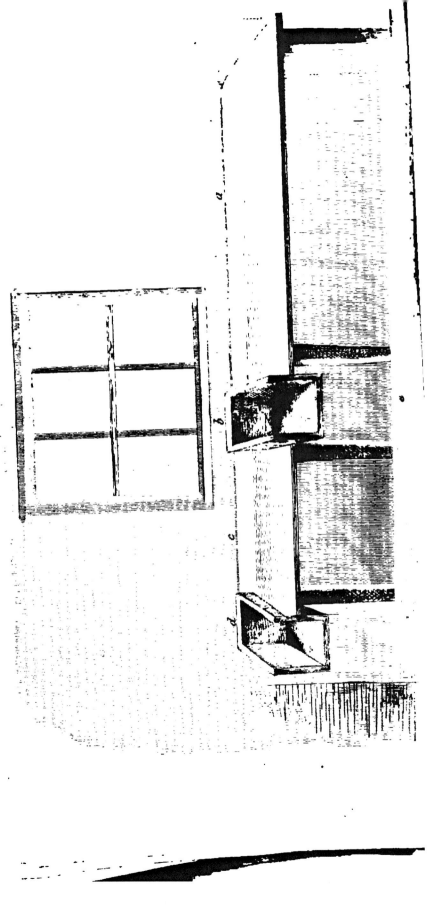

PLATE II.

CUTTING BOARDS.

CHAPTER III.

CROWN-GLASS CUTTING.

THIS is by far the most important department of the crown-glass cutter, or glazier's trade, for on its judicious performance depends a very large portion of his profits. The skilful cutter is a gainer, while the unskilful one is a grievous loser. The glass cutter must not only be able to handle his diamond well, but he must learn to cut to advantage; he must cut methodically and judiciously, that there may be as little waste as possible.

We shall attempt to describe the best methods of doing so, in as clear and perspicuous a manner as possible.

In the first place, the glass cutter must provide himself with cutting boards, as delineated in Plate II. *a*, is a breaking-out board, seven feet long, three feet broad, and two feet nine inches high, that is, high enough to strike the upper part of the thigh when the glass cutter is at work; and with a slope of from five to six inches towards the operator. *b*, is a crib fourteen inches below the level of the table, and fourteen inches wide, on which it will be found exceedingly convenient to lay ranges or corner pieces, and this without the slightest interruption to the work going forward. The cross-cutting board is three feet long, by three feet broad, for cutting up and squaring the ranges and corners; the top, one foot in breadth, being level to lay squares on when cut, of the same height, and sloped in the same manner as the breaking-out board, with a crib, of the same dimensions as that already described to place squares on edge at either side of the crib, for assorting and packing. *e*, is a board running the whole length of the cutting board, and about eighteen inches in height, which forms a convenient place for depositing the cullet or broken glass. Some glass cutters use a flat or level cutting board, and others cover it with a cloth or carpet. The sloped board is preferred by the experienced cutter, as it is easier stretched over; but probably the flat table with a cloth is best suited to the less practised workman. The cloth, however, should be used when large or fine picture glasses are to be

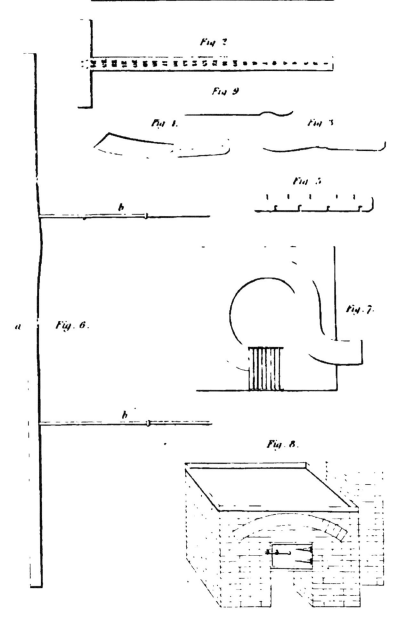

Fig. 1

Fig. 2

Fig. 9

Fig. 4   Fig. 3

Fig. 5

Fig. 6   Fig. 7

Fig. 8

cut, as they are liable to be scratched by particles of glass or sand, if cut on the uncovered board.

For the purpose of ranging tables of glass, which is the first operation, the best instrument is a rule of fir wood, called a gauntling, fifty inches long, one and a half inch broad, and about one-eighth and one-sixteenth of an inch thick, with two pieces or slips of iron eighteen inches long attached to it, and twenty inches asunder, with a moveable catch of the same metal, having a nut and screw to admit of their being shifted at pleasure, so as to cut ranges of various breadths. The instrument alluded to will be better understood, however, from Fig. 6, Plate III. *a*, is the wood; *b b*, are the two pieces of iron attached to it, very slightly made, with a small nut or screw to secure the catch on the opposite side when adjusted, and which may be altered to cut a range from six to sixteen inches broad; this instrument, though simple, is very useful, and will enable the workman to range with greater confidence, and with more safety and despatch, than he could do with the common straight edge. The cutter must also be provided with two pieces of cork, in the form of a wedge, one and a half inch thick, tapering to about one quarter of an inch, and one piece of the same size for the cross-cutter.

For cutting up bullion ranges, a small strip of white iron, three-eighths of an inch broad, may be attached to a rule at a still less expense, turned up at the ends, and adjusted to the breadth of the ranges wanted. The glass cutter ought also to be provided with a set of T squares and laths, 24, 30, and 36 inches in length, graduated by feet, inches, and fractional parts, as shewn in Figs. 1 and 2, Plate III. These instructions, with a cross-cutting board, (Plate IV.) for crosscutting, or for cutting up and squaring small or broken pieces expeditiously, are all that are necessary for ordinary purposes; but, to the extensive cutter or exporter, who requires a great variety of sizes, the breaking-out board, also indented with brass, will be found exceedingly useful, and a great saving both of time and materials.

BREAKING-OUT BOARD. *

Plate IV. shews the most approved kind at present in use. *a a* is the centre line from which the

---

* Although the sizes are figured on these reduced scales, (which is in the proportion of one-fourth to one inch,) it is not necessary that it should be so on the indented board, as it might confuse the cutter, — a little practice only is necessary to become accustomed to the lines. The cutting-board, however, should be

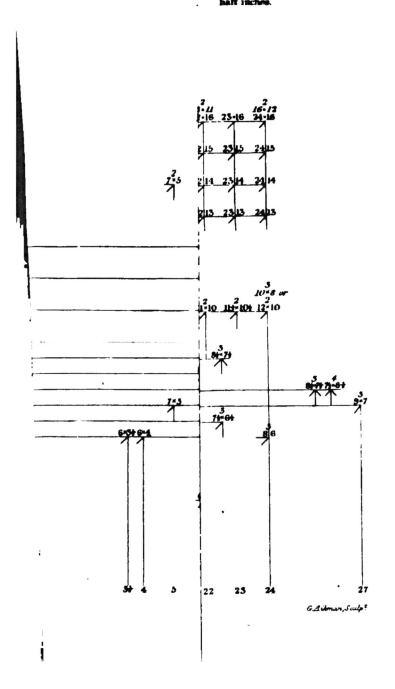

metres inches

half inches.

lengths or breadths of panes are regulated; $b\,b$ also shews the length or breadth of the panes to be cut. Apply a rule, following the lines from b to b, the extremes being 24×16, and also from the cross centre line, and the two lines will intersect each other at the point where the size of the required pane is given. To reduce this scale to practice, we shall cut up a 50 inch table; see Plate VII. Fig. 1.

Large Half.— Place the straight part of the table on a line with the lower part of the scale, on the left hand side of the table; then square a pane 15×13, taking your length 15 from the centre line; and, for greater safety and despatch, be provided with two gauntlings, one set at 17, and one at 13 inches, and, after squaring the pane to 15×13, you have from the same wing, on applying it to the scale, one 11×8, and one 6×4; you then range or rip (technically so called) the table, also applying it to the scale, at 17 inches, squaring the piece off at 23 inches; also at the left hand side, which make two $17\times11\frac{1}{2}$; and from the right hand remaining wing, also applying it to the scale, you have one 15×13, one 10×8, and one 6×4; and from the

indented with brass faintly, with half and quarter inch lines, but this could not well be shewn on the small scale.

remaining end piece you have two $6 \times 5\frac{1}{2}$, at eac.
side of the bullion.

Small Half. — Place one side of the sheet at 13
inches, and, as before described, rip up the table at
30 inches, which makes two 15×13, leaving a wing
to make one 11×9 and one 7×5; from the back
slab you have one 10×7 and two 7×5.

On cutting by this useful scale, both large and
small halves are usually begun to be cut from the
left hand; but this is not always the case, nor can
any definite rule be given for so doing, on account
of the variety of sizes and different qualities of
glass,—this must be left to the judgment and skill
of the cutter.

CROSS-CUTTING BOARD.

Plate V. represents the cross-cutting board for
cross-cutting ranges, cutting up and squaring small
pieces and breakage, or for assorting corner pieces
to their proper sizes; this scale, to the extensive
cutter or exporter, will also be found exceedingly
useful.

The black line *a* from 6 to 14 on the left hand
side of the board, is what is called a head, a small
piece of wood fixed on the board; and against this

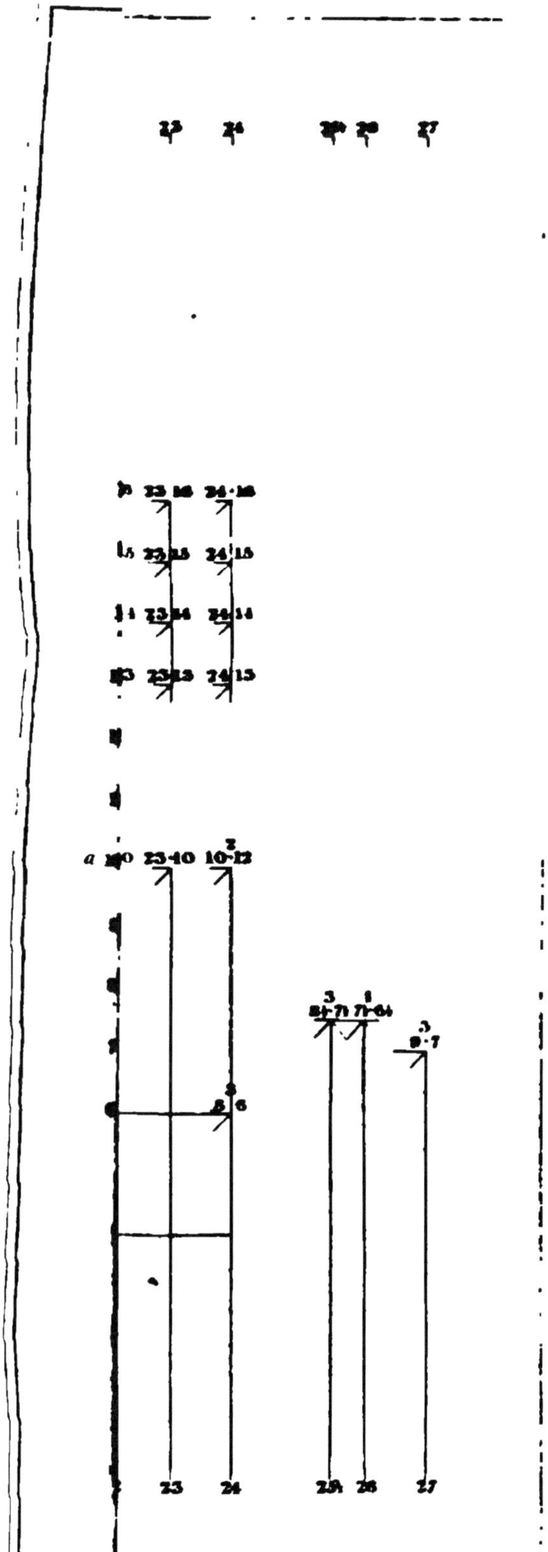

PLATE I

23 24 25 26 27

16 23.16 24.16

15 23.15 24.15

14 23.14 24.14

13 23.13 24.13

a 10 23.10 10.12

3 5
84.71 71.64

5
8.7

8.6

23 24 25 26 27

W. Cooper. Paint. del.   G. Askman sculp.

t
s

si
le
ar
of
gla
of

1
cros
piec
to tl
cutte
usefi
Tl
side
piece

head the glass about to be cut is placed to keep it square; *b b* top and bottom figures graduated from 4 to 27 inches, are the corresponding lengths or breadths of panes to be cut; in every other respect it operates in the same manner as the breaking out board described.

We shall here shew how it is used along with the breaking-out board, in cutting up large quantities with despatch; and take as an example the 50 inch table before dissected.

The cutter, after placing the table on the breaking-out board, cuts from the left hand side of the table a range to make 15×13; he hands this range to the cross-cutter, who cuts from the cross-cutting board to one pane 15×13, one 11×8, and one 6 4. The cutter then ranges, or rather rips the table at 17 inches, which he squares off at 23 inches; he hands this to the crosscutter, who cuts 2 panes, each 17×11½ inches.

The cutter also hands over the right hand wing, which the cross-cutter squares to one pane 15×15, one 10×8, and one 6×4. The bullion range is also handed to the cross-cutter, who cuts two panes 6×5½. See large half, Plate VII; the cutter at the breaking-out board proceeds in the same manner with the small half, or for any given number of panes.

useful and profitable, a great saving both in time and valuable materials; he at once sees the sizes that can be cut from any sheet, and can do so with a plain straight edge, without loss of time otherwise necessary in adjusting the graduated T squares and laths to the sizes wanted.

With regard to the selection of glass to be cut up, it may be useful to observe, —

I. Tables cut at 5 inches from the bullion, are better for country glaziers for jobbing than if cut close.

II. Tables cut close to the bullion, at $1\frac{1}{2}$, or 2 inches, or thereabouts, are calculated for the cutting of no ranges above 9 or 10 inches wide. Glass of an inferior quality should be close cut and used for smaller sizes. Sheets for large or extra sizes are also cut close.

III. Tables cut 3 to 4 inches from the bullion, are for ranges not exceeding 12 inches wide.

IV. Tables cut 5 or 6 inches from the bullion, are for ranges above 12 inches, and not exceeding 14 or $14\frac{1}{2}$ inches wide; all other squares being more properly cut from slabs.

The following are considered awkward sizes; but when glass is cut 4, 5, or 6 inches from the

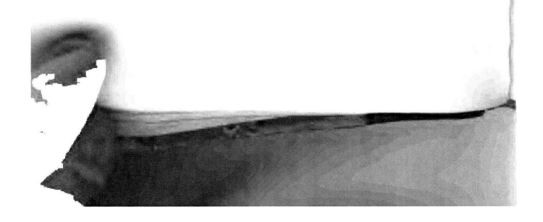

bullion, the slabs will produce the various sizes without waste; they are principally got from small halves or back slabs from 13 to 17½ inches broad: 12×12, 13×12, 14×13, 15×13, 16×14, 17×16, 18×16.

The following, which are considered regular sizes, are found among breakage, and in working up of crates, and are placed in the pigeon holes, that they may be ready when wanted. These sizes ought to be cut rough a quarter of an inch every way, except in executing an order to given dimensions, when, of course, they must be cut exact. The sizes alluded to are 10×8, 10½×8½, 11×9, 12×10, 14×10, 15×10, 15×11, 16×12, 17×12, 18×12, 18×14, or half an inch more each way.

All sizes under 10×8, must be cut rough one half inch each way; all others a quarter of an inch, excepting where a ready sale for corners can be commanded, or when they are used for half panes, or jobbing work, in which form they may be assorted to cut sizes, such as 10×8, 9×7, 8×6, 6×4, 6×3, 5×3, 4×3, or half an inch more or less each way. The cross-cutting board will assist in assorting these to their various sizes speedily, and with accuracy.

Although Plate IV. shews at once the size of panes that may be cut from tables or slabs of any size, it may be useful for the less experienced glass cutter to know the sizes most frequently cut from slabs of various dimensions, taking a 49 inch table as an average.

A 17 inch slab, * or table cut at 8 inches, will cut

      2 panes 15 × 12, or
      2   .   16 × 10, or
      2   .   17 × 10

These slabs are very useful for jobbing work.

————

An 18 inch slab, or table cut at 7 inches, will cut

      3 panes 12 × 10, or
      2   .   15 × 13, or
      2   .   16 × 12

These slabs are generally left to cut the sizes they will make, such as 28 × 12, or 26 × 13 inches.

* A 17 inch slab, &c. means that the slab measures 17 inches across the centre; and cut at 4, 5, or 6 inches, that the table is slit up or cut at that distance from the bullion, or bull's eye, being the knot or centre of the sheet; the sizes enumerated, exclusive of corner pieces, may be cut from the various slabs.

A 19 inch slab, or table, cut at 6 inches, will cut
3 panes 12×10, or
2   .   14×10, and 1, 11×9, or
2   .   15×13, or
2   .   16×12, or
1   .   16×12, 1, 14×10, and 1, 12×10

———

A 20 inch slab, or table, cut at 5 inches, will cut
1 pane 13×12, 1, 16×12, and 1, 12×12, or
1   .   14×10, and 2, 12×10, or
2   .   18×12, or
2   .   17×13, or
1   .   18×13, and 1, 16×13

———

A 21 inch slab, or table, cut at 4 inches, will cut
3 panes 12×12, and 1, 11×9, or
1   .   13×12, 2, 12×12, and 1, 12×8, or
2   .   14×12, 1, 12×8, and 1, 11×9, or
1   .   15×11, 1, 14×11, and 2, 11×9, or
1   .   18×13, and 1, 17×13, or
2   .   17×14, or
2   .   18×13, or
1   .   18×14, and 1, 16×14

A 22 inch slab, or table, cut at 3 inches, will cut

1 pane 13×12, 2, 12×12, and 1, 12×9

4 . 14×10, or

3 . 15×11, or

1 . 15×13, 2, 14×10, and 1, 12×10, or

2 . 18×14, or

1 . 20×14, and 1, 18×12

———

A 23 inch slab or table, cut at 2 inches, will cut,

3 panes 14×10, and 1, 15×12, or

1 — 15×12, 2, 14×11, and 1, 14×10, or

2 — 18×15.

———

Crown-glass always cuts best in a warm temperature. When it happens to be hard, which is seldom the case, (a bad diamond, or not knowing how to use a good one, being the usual cause of breakage,) it has been found to cut better after warming the glass before the fire, which has the effect of diminishing the tension of the ill annealed glass.

The following shew the quantity of saleable glass to be cut from tables of 48, 49, 50, and 51 inches diameter, sizes usually found in crates, and exclusive of 5×3, and 4×3.

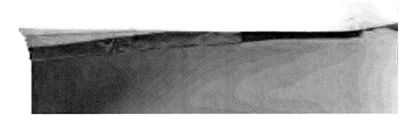

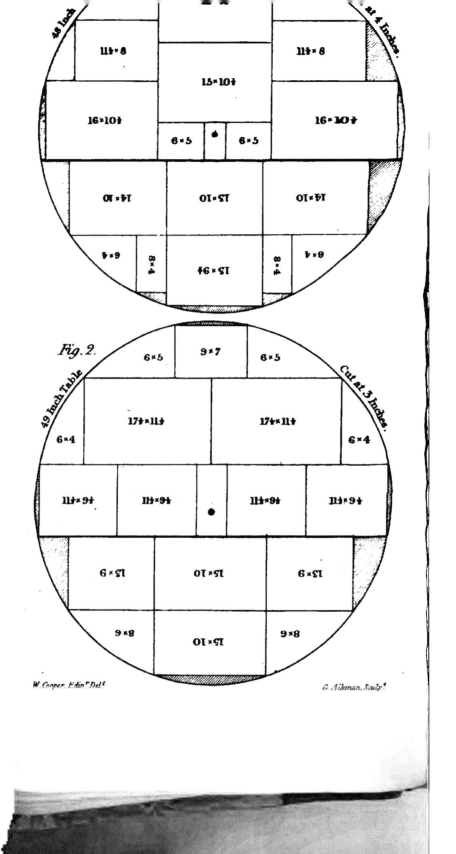

Fig. 2.

49 Inch Table

Cut at 3 Inches.

W. Cooper, Edin.r Del.t   G. Aikman, Sculp.t

48 Inch Table, PLATE VI, Fig. 1.

Large Half.

			Ft.	In.
2 panes	16	×10½	2	48
1 .	15	×11	1	21
1 .	15	×10½	1	13
2 .	11½	×8	1	40
2 .	6½	×5	0	65
2 .	6	×5	0	60

Ft. In.
6 103

Small Half.

			Ft.	In.
2 panes	14	×10	1	136
1 .	13	×10	0	130
1 .	13	× 9½	0	123½
2 .	8	× 4	0	64
2 .	6	× 4	0	48

4 69

Saleable glass cut from a 48 inch table. .   .

Ft. In.
11 28

49 Inch Table, PLATE VI, Fig. 2.

Large Half.

			Ft.	In.
2 panes	17½	×11½	2	115
4 .	11½	× 9¼	3	6
1 .	9	× 7	0	63
2 .	6	× 5	0	60
2 .	6	× 4	0	48

Ft. In.
7 4

Small Half.

			Ft.	In.
2 panes	15	×10	2	12
2 .	13	× 9	1	90
2 .	8	× 6	0	96

4 54

Saleable glass cut from a 49 inch table, .   .

Ft. In.
11 59

50 Inch Table, PLATE VII, Fig. 1.

Large Half.

		Ft.	In.
2 panes	15×13	2	102
2 .	17×11½	2	103
1 .	11× 8	0	88
1 .	10× 8	0	80
2 .	6× 4	0	48
2 .	6 × 5½	0	66

Ft. In.
——— 7 55

Small Half.

		Ft.	In.
2 panes	15×13	2	102
1 .	11× 9	0	99
2 .	7× 5	0	70
2 .	6× 5	0	60
1 .	10× 7	0	70

——— 4 113

Saleable glass cut from a 50 inch
table   .   .

Ft. In.
——— 12 24

51 Inch Table, PLATE VII, Fig. 2.

Large Half.

		Ft.	In.
2 panes	22 ×14½	4	102
1 .	18½×16	2	8
2 .	11 × 8	1	32
2 .	6 × 5	0	60
1 .	6 × 4	0	24
1 .	8 × 4 bullion	0	32

Ft. In.
——— 8 114

Small Half.

		Ft.	In.
2 panes	16½×13½	3	14
2 .	7 × 5½	0	77
2 .	7 × 5	0	70

——— 4 17

Saleable glass cut from a 51 inch
table,   .   .

Ft. In.
——— 12 131

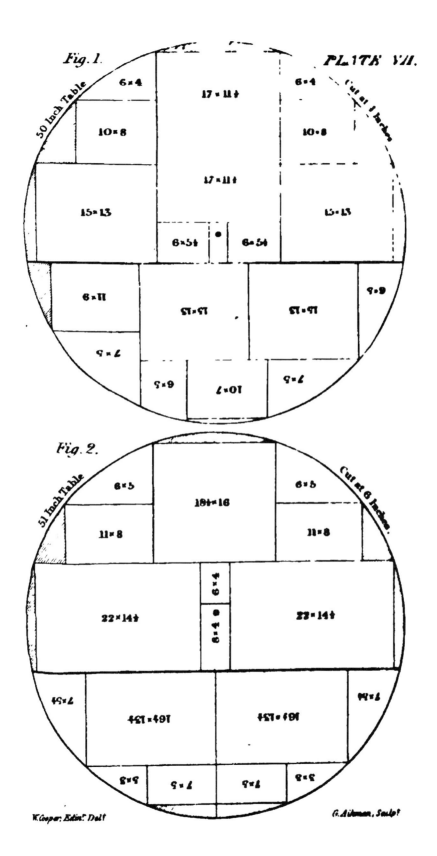

Fig. 1.   PLATE VII.

Fig. 2.

W. Cooper, Edinʳ Delt   G. Aikman, Sculpᵗ

PLATE VIII.

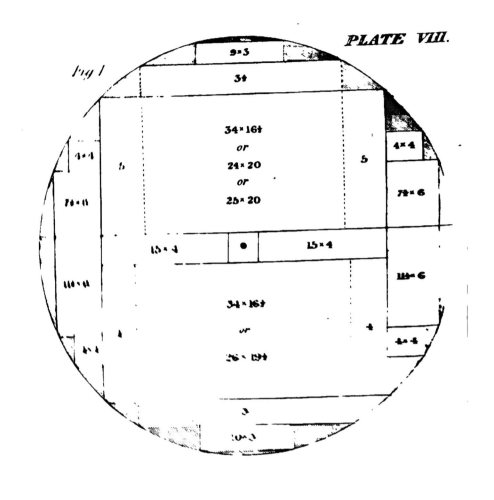

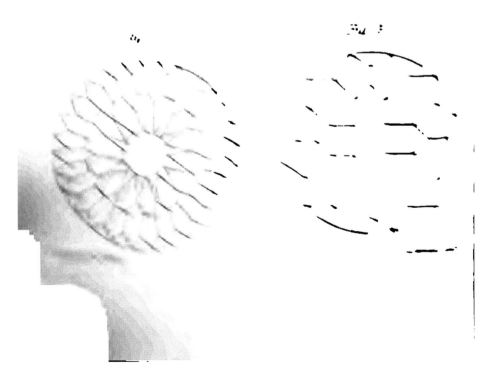

PLATE VIII. FIG. 1, shews the largest panes, &c. cut from a Table 50 inches diameter, close cut.

Large Half.			Ft.	In.
1 pane 34	×	16½	3	129
2 . 15	×	4	0	120
1 . 26	×	3	0	78
2 . 11½	×	6	0	138
2 . 4	×	4	0	32
1 . 10	×	3	0	30
			6	95

Or,				
1 pane 26	×	19½	3	75
2 . 16	×	4	0	132
2 . 11½	×	6	0	138
2 . 4	×	4	0	32
2 . 15	×	4	0	120
1 . 10	×	3	0	30
			6	95

Small Half.			Ft.	In.
1 pane 34	×	16½	3	129
1 . 24	×	3½	0	84
2 . 7½	×	6	0	90
2 . 4	×	4	0	32
1 . 9	×	3	0	27
			5	74

Or,				
1 pane 24	×	20	3	48
2 . 16½	×	5	1	21
2 . 7½	×	6	0	90
2 . 4	×	4	0	32
1 . 9	×	3	0	27
			5	74

	Ft.	In.
	12	25
Waste in cutting, . .	1	66
Round contents of a Table		
50 inches diameter,	13	91

D

The produce of tables of given diameters, will differ in quantity according to the sizes of panes to be cut; and these are so various, that no fixed number of feet for practical use can be given.

The following table shews the average quantity of saleable glass to be cut from the various sizes of tables, and exclusive of 5×3, and 4×3:

Diameter of tables.	Contents.	Saleable glass to be cut from each crate.		
		12s.	15s.	18s.
48	12½	134½	168	201
49	13	140	175	210
50	13½	146	182½	219
51	14	152	190	228

PLATE VIII. FIG. 1. In reference to this figure, it is not asserted that a 50 inch table will in all cases contain 13 feet 91 inches superficial, as tables are seldom found circular; but a 50 inch table will contain nearly that quantity, for what is deficient on one side of the table, is usually made up by the other side being so much larger. This figure is meant to shew the largest panes to be cut from a table 50 inches diameter, and the squares to be cut from what remains over. The cutter might have tables drawn in the same manner to various sizes of tables, such as 49, 49½, 50, 50½, 51, 51½, 52, &c.

PLATE IX, which we shall call the crown-glass Theodolite, shews at one view the largest panes that can be cut from tables of given diameters. The curved lines describe the quadrant of circles of tables, from 48 to 64 inches diameter, being the largest size of crown glass now manufactured.

The top and bottom graduated lines, *a a*, shew the length, and the end lines, *b b*, the breadth of the required panes; and these lines intersect each other at the edge of the table which it takes to cut such panes. To find the largest panes, therefore, to be cut from a full half sheet or table of glass, of course the top and bottom lines are doubled, as they only represent one-half the diameter—the numbers being taken from the centre of the sheet. For example, what size of a table does it take to cut a pane 30 × 20 inches? Look for 15 on the lines *a a*, (which, being doubled, is 30,) and for 20 on the lines *b b*, and immediately, on the intersecting lines on the circle, you have 53 inches, size of a table required to cut a pane 30 × 20. It must also be kept in view here, that tables of glass are not always perfectly circular. This diagram is only intended to give an idea of the plan to the practical glass-cutter, who may have the same drawn to the full size, with the intersecting lines at quarter

and half inches,—to shew which, would
small a scale. It is understood, though
diameters of tables are marked on the cur
that the table or sheet of glass is calculated
cut or slit at one and one-half inches fi
bullion, or, which is the same thing, at tw
from the centre of the bullion. From this d
we learn, that

A 50 inch half table

will make panes	33 × 17	31 × 18	28 × 19	25
51	—	33 × 18	30 × 19	27 × 20	23
52	—	34 × 18	32 × 19	29 × 20	26
53	—	33 × 19	30 × 20	28 × 21	24
54	—	34 × 19	32 × 20	30 × 21	27
55	—	34 × 20	32 × 21	28 × 22	26 ×
56	—	35 × 20	33 × 21	30 × 22	27 ×
57	—	35 × 21	32 × 22	29 × 23	26 ×
58	—	36 × 21	33 × 22	31 × 23	28 ×
59	—	35 × 22	33 × 23	30 × 24	27 ×
60	—	37 × 22	35 × 23	32 × 24	29 ×

The following theorem may give a pretty good
idea of the number of available feet to be cut from
a table of glass; although, as has been already
observed, tables of given diameters vary in thickness and weight.

2

CRITI...

hich m...

stood ...

d on th...

is calcu...

lf inc...

hing, ...

From ...

$28 \times 1...$

$17 \times 1...$

$9 \times 2...$

$\times 21...$

$\times 21...$ *b*

$\vdots 21...$

$\vdots$

3

9

75

k

u

t

Suppose the average weight of a 50 inch table to be 9 lb.

A crate of 12 tables will weigh 108 lb.

Take the number of feet which a table of 50 inches diameter contains, which is 13½ feet nearly;

A crate of 12 tables will produce 162 feet.

The cullet or waste arising from the cutting of crates into squares, exclusive of the squares 4 × 3 and 5 × 3, averages nearly 2 lb. per table.

In a crate of 12 tables there will be 24 lb.

Well, then, take the average weight of 100 feet of glass, 63 lb.

Then, if 63 lb. produce 100 feet, how many feet will 24 lb. produce?

Ft.   lb.   lb.

As 100 : 63 :: 24

24

100 ⌐1512⌐ 15 feet waste in 12 tables.

Available glass, ... 147 feet*

Waste, ... 15

Round contents of a 12 table crate, 50 inches diameter, . . . 162 feet.

* See Plate VII. Fig. 1, produce of one table × 12.

CHAPTER IV.

PACKING OF GLASS.

In packing panes of crown-glass, care should be taken to have the boxes in which they are to be packed of such a size as that no more space shall be left than is necessary to introduce the hay or other materials with which they are to be secured.

By attending to this consideration, not only is a saving of wood effected, but a greater degree of safety ensured for the glass during its transit.

The best material for packing is meadow hay; and this should be pretty frequently intervened between the naked panes, as placing too many together without the intervention of some soft substance, greatly endangers their safety. Of such panes as 6×4, 7×5, 8×6, 9×7, to 10×8, a dozen may be laid together; and of such as 10×8 to 12×10, half a dozen; of 14×12 to 16×12 five; of from 16×12, to about 20×14, four; and from 20×12 to 24×16, not more than two or three panes should be laid together, observing, to ensure safety in the carriage, that in the quantities named, the panes lie close to one another, packing separately such panes as are bent or twisted.

It may not be unnecessary to mention here, that a dozen panes, when in close contact with one another, occupy nearly the space of an inch in thickness.

The hay, or packing material, whatever it may be, ought to be well and firmly stuffed around the glass, after it is deposited in the box; and this will be most easily and effectually accomplished by a simple piece of wood of the shape represented in Plate III. Fig. 9. which can be made for the purpose in a few minutes.

To each end of the box a handle of rope-yarn should be attached, for greater convenience in removing it from place to place; but care must be taken that the holes perforated in the end of the box through which the rope-yarn is passed, be not on a line with each other, but as represented in Plate X. Fig. 9; otherwise, if the boxes be made of fir, as they generally are, *the piece between the two holes,* placed on a line, would be apt to come away, and the glass be thus broken to pieces by the fall which would necessarily ensue. The two ends of the rope-yarn handles are secured inside by a knot thrown on each; and these knots must be provided with a corresponding hollow in the wood, excavated for their reception, to prevent their coming in contact with the glass, which they might break; or the handles may be spliced outside, and sunk into a hollow cut by a gouge on the end of the box, of a depth sufficient to cover the rope ; which would occupy less space in stowage, and consequently be a saving of freight.

Fifty and a hundred feet are the usual quantities packed into one box ; but of small sizes, two hundred feet may be put into one box, the squares being packed on the top of each other. In this case, however, the latter should be provided with a board or support on the top of the first layer. Figures 11, 12, and 14, only are made in this form.

In calculating the size of the box or boxes required, it is usual to allow about one or one and a half inches each way, over and above the length and breadth of the pane, for the length and depth of the box, and to allow farther one-eighth of an inch on each pane for the breadth of the box ; these allowances are made for hay and inside measure.

The annexed table shews the proper sizes of 50, 100, and 200 feet boxes — the contents of each pane, — the number of panes per 100 feet — the proper thickness of wood employed in making boxes, and where the divisions ought to occur.

PLATE X.

50 Feet Boxes.

100 Feet Boxes.

End.

200 Feet Boxes.

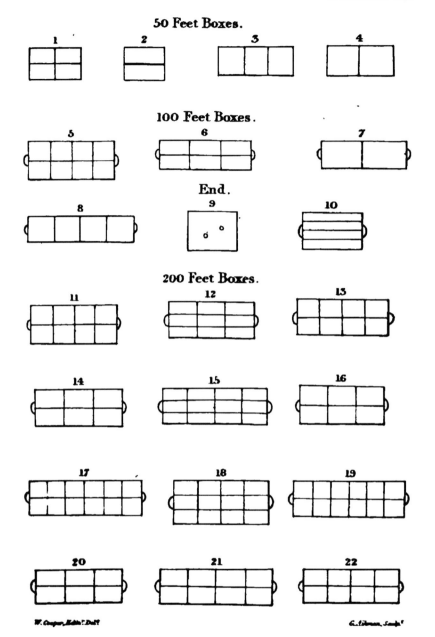

Sizes of Panes.	Contents of 1 Pane.			No. of Panes in 100 Feet.		50 Feet Boxes.				100 Feet Boxes.				200 Feet Boxes.			
	Feet.	Inches.	Parts.	Dozens.	Panes.	Length.	Width.	Depth.	Shape.	Length.	Width.	Depth.	Shape.	Length.	Width.	Depth.	Shape.
						In.	In.	In.	Pl. 10	In.	In.	In.	Pl. 10	In.	In.	In.	Pl. 10
3 × 4	0	1	0	100	0	0	0	0		26	15	5		26	15	10½	Fig.
3 × 5	0	1	3	80	0	0	0	0		22	15	6	Fig. 5	22	15	12½	13
3 × 6	0	1	6	66	8	0	0	0		23½	12	7		23½	12	14½	12
4 × 6	0	2	0	50	0	13	10	7		26	10	7		27	14	10½	13
4½ × 6	0	2	3	44	6	12	11	7		25	11	7		25½	14	11½	
4½ × 6½	0	2	5	41	1	12	11	7½		24	11	7½		23	14	12½	14
4 × 7	0	2	4	42	11	12½	10	8	Fig. 1	24½	10	8		31	15	8	
4½ × 7	0	2	7	38	2	12	10	8		24	11	8		28	16½	8	18
5 × 6	0	2	6	40	0	12	12	7		24	12	7		23	14	12½	20
5½ × 6	0	2	9	36	6	21	7	6½		21	13	7		36	13	7	17
5½ × 6½	0	2	11	33	7	21	7½	6½		21	14	7	Fig. 6	36	14	7	
5 × 7	0	2	11	34	4	21	8	6		21	12	8		26	18	8	15
5½ × 7	0	3	2	31	3	20	8	6½		20	13	8		35	13	8	
5½ × 7½	0	3	5	29	2	18	8½	6½	Fig. 3	18	13	8½		34	13	8½	17
6 × 6	0	3	0	33	4	20	7	7		20	14	7		22	14	14½	
6½ × 6½	0	3	6	28	5	18	7½	7½		18	15	7½		18	15	15½	16
6 × 7	0	3	6	28	7	18	8	7		18	14	8		34	14	8	17
Quarries 9s	0	0	0	0	0	0	0	0		22	10	9	Fig. 7				
6 × 8	0	4	0	25	0	15	9	7		30	9	7		30	14	9	
6½ × 7½	0	4	0	24	8	15	8½	7½		30	15	8½		30	15	8½	
7 × 9	0	5	3	19	0	13	10	8	Fig. 4	25	10	8		25	16	10	
7½ × 8½	0	5	3	18	11	13	9½	8½		25	9½	8½		24	17	9½	
8 × 10	0	6	8	15	0	11	11	9		22	11	9		22	18	11	
8½ × 9½	0	6	8	14	11	10½	11	9½		22	10½	9½	Fig. 8	21	19	10½	21
9 × 11	0	8	3	12	2	12	10½	10		21	12	10		21	10	12	
9 × 12	0	9	0	11	2	13	10	10		20	13	10		20	20	13	
9 × 13	0	9	9	10	4	14	10	10		19	14	10		19	20	14	
10 × 12	0	10	0	10	0	13	9½	11		19	13	11		19	22	13	
10 × 13	0	10	10	9	3	14	9	11		14½	16	11					
10 × 14	0	11	8	8	7	15	8	11		15½	16	11					
10 × 15	1	0	6	8	0	16½	7½	11		16½	15	11					
10 × 16	1	1	4	7	6	17	7½	11		17½	14	11					
11 × 13	0	11	11	8	5	14	8	12		14½	15	12					
11 × 14	1	0	10	7	10	15	7½	12		15½	14½	12					
11 × 15	1	1	9	7	4	16	7½	12		16½	14	12					
11 × 16	1	2	8	6	10	17	7	12		17½	14	12					
11 × 17	1	3	7	6	5	18	7	12		18½	13½	12					
11 × 18	1	4	6	6	1	19	7	12		19½	13½	12					
12 × 14	1	2	0	7	2	15	7	13		15½	14	13					
12 × 15	1	3	0	6	8	16½	7	13		16	14	13					
12 × 16	1	4	0	6	3	17½	6½	13		17½	13	13					
12 × 17	1	5	0	5	11	18½	6½	13	Fig. 2	18½	12½	13					
12 × 18	1	6	0	5	7	19½	6	13		19½	12	13					
12 × 19	1	7	0	5	4	20½	6	13		20½	11½	13					
12 × 20	1	8	0	5	0	21½	6	13		21½	11½	13	Fig. 10				
13 × 15	1	4	3	6	2	16½	7	14		16½	13	14					
13 × 16	1	5	4	5	10	17½	6½	14		17½	12½	14					
13 × 17	1	6	5	5	6	18½	6	14		18½	12	14					
13 × 18	1	7	6	5	2	19½	6	14		19½	12	14					
13 × 19	1	8	7	4	11	20½	6	14		20½	11½	14					
13 × 20	1	9	8	4	8	21½	6	14		21½	11½	14					
13 × 21	1	10	9	4	5	22½	6	14		22½	11	14					
14 × 16	1	6	8	5	5	17½	6	15		17½	12	15					
14 × 18	1	9	0	4	10	19½	6	15		19½	11½	15					
14 × 20	1	11	4	4	4	21½	6	15		21½	11	15					
14 × 21	2	0	6	4	1	22½	6	15		22½	11	15					
14 × 22	2	1	8	3	11	23½	6	15		23½	11	15					
15 × 20	2	1	0	4	0	21½	6	16		21½	11½	16					
15 × 22	2	3	6	3	8	23½	6	16		23½	11	16					
16 × 22	2	5	4	3	5	23½	6	17		23½	11	17					
16 × 24	2	8	0	3	2	25½	6	17		25½	11	17					

These are the proper sizes when neatly packed with soft meadow hay. One inch, or half an inch more each way may be allowed by the less experienced packer.

The wood for 50 feet boxes to be five-eighth inch at the sides, and three-fourth inch for the ends. For 100 feet boxes three-fourth inch sides, and one inch ends. For 200 feet boxes, one inch wood round and round.

To find how many squares there are in 100 square feet of any given size,

Multiply 144, number of square inches in a foot, by 100, and divide by the square contents of the pane.

EXAMPLE.

How many panes in one hundred square feet.

144
100
———

Size 22½ × 16 = 360)14400(40 squares in 100 ft.
                    14400   22½ × 16
                    ———

CHAPTER V.

GLAZING OF WINDOWS.

In this part of the work, it is meant to be as practical as possible, and we shall therefore, without hesitation, sacrifice niceties of language, and all similar considerations, to brevity and perspicuity. Our great object here, as it has been throughout, is to convey our information in as distinct and intelligible a manner as possible.

Before proceeding to speak of glazing, the order in which its various processes present themselves naturally demands that we should say something of

PUTTY.

This important and indispensable article in the glazier's trade, is composed of whiting and linseed oil. Chalk is sometimes used instead of the former, but the expense and labour incurred in preparing it is so much greater, that it can be no object to the glazier to employ it; for although it is certainly cheaper in the first instance, it will not ultimately be found so. Besides, the glazier will find it almost impossible to free it so completely of the sand and silica, with which it abounds, as to render it fit for making good putty. These will remain in such abundance, as to endanger the safety of the glass in working it in; neither will the putty work kindly or well.

Whiting being therefore, in every way, to be preferred, it must be thoroughly dried before the oil is added to it, otherwise the union will not be effected, or at least be very imperfect.

Figs. 7 and 8, Plate III. represent a kiln for drying and preparing whiting; and we do not know that any simpler, more economical, or more effective method could be employed.

This kiln will dry a ton of whiting per day, at a very trifling expense of fuel,* and the kiln itself, with all its erections, will probably not cost more than fifty shillings. Every glazier, therefore, whose business is of any extent, ought to be provided with one of them.

Fig. 7, Plate III. shews the ground plan of a whiting kiln. The grate room may be twelve by

* The wood of one empty crate will dry whiting to glaze three 18 table crates.

ten inches, with an ash pit one foot in depth. The flue, as shewn in the plan, branches from the side of the fire place in a circular form, for the purpose of distributing the heat equally on the plate, and discharges itself into the adjoining vent.

Fig. 8, Plate III. is an elevation of the kiln, about three feet square, on the top of which the cast iron plate, of the same dimensions, and half an inch in thickness, is placed, with raised sides, to keep the whiting from falling over while stirring it occasionally, to prevent its being overheated, or burned; in which case it will require more oil, and produce less putty. It ought not to be quite cold when wrought into putty; the oil should be added while the whiting still retains a very slight degree of heat. It will then expand, and consequently saturate a greater quantity of whiting, and with less labour, too, than when cold; and thus, of course, produce a proportionately greater quantity of putty.

In cases where the glazier has no such kiln for drying his whiting as that above described, he may produce the desired result on a small scale, by pulverizing newly slacked lime, say in the proportion of a piece about the size of an egg, to a hundred weight of whiting, and mixing them together. This method of drying whiting is perfectly effective, and

answers very well where the business is not extensive; but it is a tedious process, and is only adapted
for small quantities.

After the whiting has been thoroughly dried and
prepared, it ought to be passed through a very fine
sieve, and all the lumps and knots that remain
pulverized with a three inch roller on a table; and
then also passed through the sieve. Great care
must be taken to keep the whiting free of sand and
other extraneous substances; the former, in particular, is extremely injurious to putty.

When putty is to be made, put the proper quantity of oil into a tub or other open vessel, (the one
half of an oil pipe answers extremely well for the
purpose,) and gradually add the whiting, at the
same time keeping the whole in motion, with a stout
stick fashioned like an oar, until it becomes of a
sufficient consistency to work by the hand on a
board or table. Having been removed thither from
the tub, it must be wrought up with dry whiting,
until it is converted into a solid compact mass.
When brought to this state, it ought to be put into
a hollowed stone or mortar, and beat with a wooden
mallet till it becomes soft and tenacious, when more
whiting must be added, until it has attained a proper
consistency.

It is considered that the putty is improved, if the whiting and oil, after being mixed, are allowed to remain for about twenty hours before being wrought up. After putty has been made, it should be firmly packed in a cask, from which it may be taken from time to time, as it is required. It ought not to be used for ten or twelve days after it is made, when its colour, from having at first been a dull yellow, will have changed to a whitish free stone, which renders it more suitable for most purposes, from its being of a less conspicuous tint.

After a lapse of six or eight weeks, the putty in the cask will become hard; but it is easily restored to its original softness, by being beat as before, and it is much improved by this second operation.

Putty is made in England in large quantities, and is ground in a mill in the same way as white lead; but this is no improvement, as it is generally over-wrought in this method of preparation, and rendered so tough and tenacious, that it does not work well, and is entirely without that degree of pliability which putty ought to possess.

The glazier, therefore, will himself make a much more *workable* putty with his mortar and mallet, and fully as cheaply, by employing his apprentices in its manufacture at their leisure hours.

When putty of a superior degree of fineness, which will dry quickly, is required, add a little sugar of lead, or litharge; and if an increase of strength be wanted, a little white lead.

We now proceed to

GLAZING.

To glaze well, neatly, and expeditiously, simple as the operation may appear, is an art not to be acquired in a day. On the contrary, several years of practice are necessary, before that degree of proficiency in it, which constitutes an efficient and expert glazier, is acquired.

When a glazier receives an order to glaze a house, the first thing he must do, of course, is to proceed to measure the work to be done. In doing this, he must take the *full* size of the panes, that enough may be left for stripping, so as to produce an accurate fit into the sashes. This fitting must be performed with great care and nicety, leaving about one thirty-second part of an inch of space on each side and end of the pane, between it and the check. In other words, the pane must fill the space appropriated for it, to within the thirty-second part of an inch, or thereabouts.

This space is left to provide for such occurrences

as the wood swelling with moisture, or the building setting, in which cases the panes would be apt to crack.

When the panes have been fitted into the checks of the sashes in the manner spoken of, they must be removed, and the checks well bedded with beat putty. This done, the panes are again returned to their respective places, and gently pressed or lodged into the bedding, humouring the glass as it were, should it be bent or twisted, and taking care that there is no hard extraneous substance mingled with the putty, which might endanger, if not actually break the glass.

When a pane is perfectly bedded, it lies quite firm, and does not spring from the putty; but when, either from a perverse bend or twist in the glass, or any other accidental cause, it happens that it cannot be made to go quite close to the check, the vacant space must be carefully and neatly filled upon the back puttying, otherwise the window will not be impervious to the weather, and will be very apt to fall into decay by the admission of moisture.

It may not be superfluous to observe here, that the convex, or round side of the pane, where such a shape occurs, should be presented to the outside, and the concave or hollow to the inside. The reasons for recommending this disposition of such

E

panes are so obvious that they need hardly be enumerated. It may, however, be stated generally, that, when thus placed, they resist the weather better than if the hollow sides were exposed to it.

After the pane has been bedded, the next process is the outside puttying. This putty should be kept in the fore cheek, about the thirty-second part of an inch below the level of the inside cheek, so as to allow the thin layer of paint which binds these two substances together, to join the putty and glass; and that it may not offend the eye by being seen from the inside; and that, when it is painted, the brush may not encroach on any visible part of the pane, leaving those ragged lines or marks which are so often seen from the inside on ill-finished windows, and which are so displeasing to the eye. This operation, and finishing the corners, are two nice points in the art, and therefore, when properly done, discover at once the neat-handed and skilful tradesman.

It is the opinion of some experienced glaziers, that the inside puttying, which is the next process, ought to be allowed to remain eight days before being finished off, while others, again, say that this should be immediately done. The experience of the writer inclines him to the former opinion. By standing over for some little time, the putty acquires a hardness which admits of a better and neater finish than when it is in the soft working state, and in this way also, the putty is not liable to shrink. Of course, this is only recommended in cases of extensive jobs. When only a few panes are done, it is better to finish them off at once, than subject the employers to the inconvenience of a second visit from the glazier for so trifling a purpose.

When the finishing does take place, however, the putty must be cut clean off with the putty knife, and on a level with the style of the astragals. Complete the work by cleaning the glass and putty with a 000 duster brush, which removes all dust and loose putty from the pane, *lightly* and effectually.*

Plate III. Fig. 3, represents a glazier's putty knife; Fig. 5, a grosing iron, used for grinding or breaking off small corners, &c. when they cannot be easily cut by the diamond.

* In taking out old glass from windows, the cold putty knife, Fig. 4. Plate III. is used; but when the putty has been in the windows for ten or twelve years, it becomes nearly as hard as stone, and impenetrable to the knife. In this case there are various means used to extract the glass from the frames. The application of hot iron to the putty is sometimes adopted; but this cannot with safety be applied to the bedding, to which the glass obstinately adheres. Muriatic acid diluted with water is an excellent means of removing putty from glass, its action being

The frames or sashes of a hot-house ought, before being glazed, to receive two coats of white paint, to which a small portion of red lead has been added to facilitate its drying, and to give increased strength and durability to the paint.

The panes in the roofs of hot-houses are generally of either of the three forms exhibited in Plate XI. Figures 1, 2, and 3. The first is the square pattern, the second is the tapered, the third the semicircular.

Fig. 1, is the most generally used hitherto, and has a very good effect.

Fig. 2, is considered an improvement on No. 1, in so far as the tapered point carries off the rain down the centre of the pane, and thereby preserves the astragals; but there is a loss in shaping the glass to the tapered point.

assisted by rubbing the putty occasionally with a bit of stick. The most effectual way to remove the glass, when the frames are worthless and the glass valuable, is to put the frames into a horse dunghill, keeping the whole damp (if the weather is not so) for several weeks, which completely loosens the glass, and rots or destroys the frames.

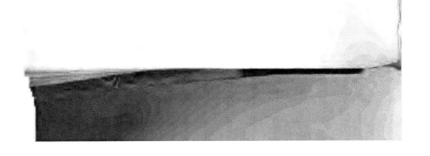

PLATE I

Fig. 1

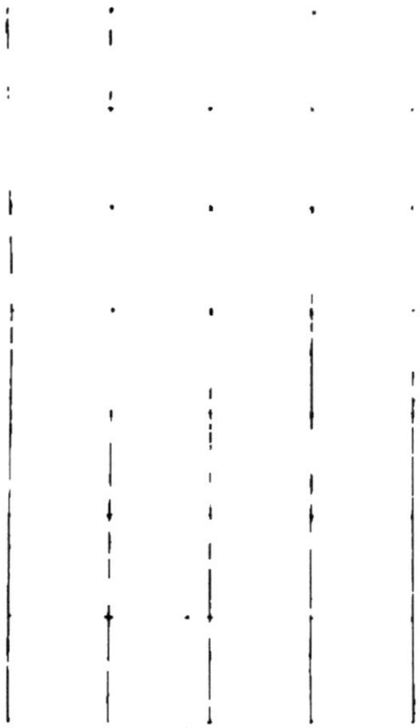

W. Cooper Edin. del.

Fig. 2

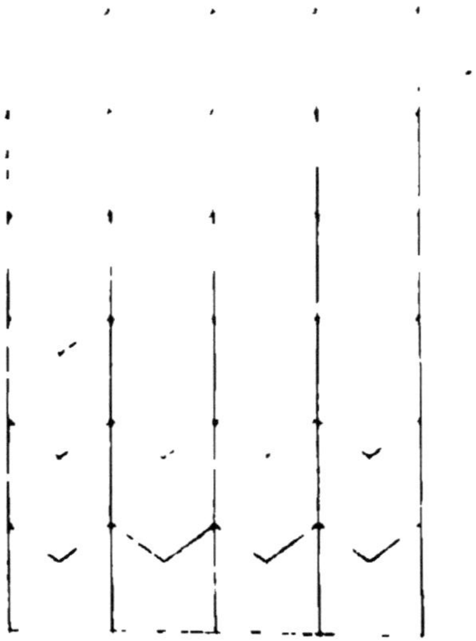

Fig. 3

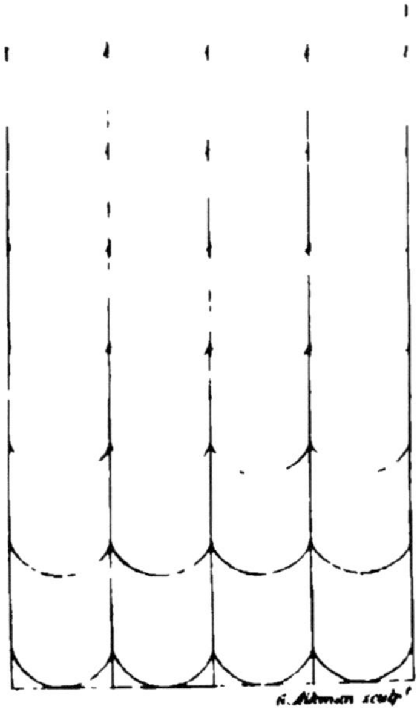

G. Aikman sculp.

Fig. 3, is decidedly the best pattern of the three — the water is not only drawn to the centre of the pane, and the astragals protected from the rain, but this pattern has a more elegant appearance, when uniformly glazed, than either of the two other shapes. There is no loss in cutting the glass to the curve, and it is therefore not more expensive.

The dimensions of hot-house panes are generally about six inches, and are made to overlay each other, to an extent regulated by the circumstance of their being puttied at the overlay or not.

If it is intended to fill in the overlays with putty, they need not be more than a quarter of an inch in depth, but if it is not intended to putty them, they must then be at least five-eighths of an inch.

The overlays, however, ought always to be puttied, and that for two reasons. First, because it will more certainly secure their being water-tight, and will, in the next place, prevent the breakage to which the panes are liable from the freezing of the water, or moisture, which lodges in the overlay, and which, thereby expanding, instantly shivers the glass in all directions; when they are filled with putty, such an accident cannot happen.

In glazing hot-house roofs, it must be observed,

that the courses ought to run from end to end, and that the smaller panes, when such are used, should be reserved for the top.

When sashes are glazed, they ought to stand for eight or ten days before taking off the back putty, and they ought not to be painted for about three weeks afterwards, that the putty may consolidate. Great care, too, should be taken, when the sashes are newly glazed, that they be not in any way twisted or bent, as such an accident would almost inevitably start the panes from their beds, and thus render them pervious to water.

When sashes are of considerable dimensions — say about six feet by three — they should be strengthened by having two iron rods placed across them at equal distances, and screwed to the astragals. This will go far to prevent the accident of twisting, to which such frames are extremely liable, and which is very injurious to them after they have been filled with glass.

The putty used for glazing hot-houses ought to be of the very best description, as, from the circumstance of its position, it is necessarily more exposed to the action of the weather, than in the perpendicular windows.

The putty used for filling in the overlays ought

to be of a black, or lead colour, which, every glazier knows, is imparted to the putty by working lamp black into it; but as this substance has the effect of weakening the putty, the defect may be remedied by adding two pounds of white lead, ground in oil, to each stone of putty, and in a similar proportion to smaller or greater quantities. Indeed, all putty used in glazing hot-houses ought to have a portion of white lead mixed with it, as it adds greatly to its strength.

LATTICE, OR LEAD WINDOWS.

This antique and singularly beautiful style of glazing has unaccountably fallen much into disuse, although in late years it certainly has undergone something like a resuscitation, in consequence of a revival of the public taste for stained glass, and a growing predilection for Gothic architecture in churches, cottages, &c. For these, and for stair-case windows, and, indeed, all windows similarly situated, as in halls, lobbies, or the like, it is peculiarly adapted.

It may be proper to premise, that lead windows require stained or coloured glass for producing their

fullest and best effects, and it was with stained
glass only that they were originally constructed;
but very neat and elegant windows are executed
in this style with plain glass, where variety and
beauty of figure are made to compensate for the
absence of colour. It is thought that the glazier
would find it for his advantage to turn more of his
attention to this very elegant branch of his art, than
he has hitherto done.

Lead windows may be made to any pattern, and
in this there is great scope for the display of a
correct taste.   In the time of Elizabeth, this branch
of the glazier's art was carried to great excellence,
especially by one Walter Gedde, who was employed
in glazing most of the royal and public buildings of
that period. This person executed in this style
some windows of transcendent beauty, displaying
an endless variety of the most elegant and elaborate
figures.

The most useful and most common description of
plain glass lead windows, however, are those of the
diamond or lozenge shape ; but, as already said, they
may be made to any pattern desired.   Annexed are
various specimens of windows done in this style,
including that to which we have just now more
particularly alluded.

Plate XII. is the east window of St Giles' Church, Edinburgh. *

Plate XIII. is a very simple pattern, easily cut, and forming a neat, cheap, and durable window for a staircase, if the diamond panes were stained, and the remainder frosted glass.

Plate XIV. is more ornamental; and although apparently more elaborate, the glass is easily cut, by forming the pattern as directed in a following part of this article. This window has a beautiful effect by introducing stained glass into the long skittle shaped pieces, and in the rosette in the centre.

Plate VIII. Fig. 2, is well calculated for the bull's-eye of a large Gothic window, or a circular light, in any style of architecture. It has a beautiful effect in colours, particularly if a handsome rosette is inserted in the centre.

Plate VIII. Fig. 3, called St Catherine's Wheel is a good common pattern, and looks well, if the stained glass is properly contrasted. Both this and the last, when divided in the centre, make good fan-lights.

* The whole of this splendid Gothic edifice was reconstructe by William Burn, Esq. architect, Edinburgh, in 1832. Th window is wrought in the diamond or lozenge shape, which is most general use at present.

introduced here, is a better method of leading a window in common glass, than the usual diamond shaped pieces. The small quarries should be filled with stained glass, and thus a very neat window will be formed.

Plate XV. Fig. 2, is a fan-light, which, if properly varied with stained glass, will have a beautiful effect, either in Grecian or Gothic architecture.

Plate XVI. is divided into large compartments, but not too large to be held together by leading. This pattern will look very well even in plain glass, but will have a beautiful effect when the small squares are filled with handsome stained glass rosettes —the other part of the window frosted, or, perhaps, stained glass, and the centre of the diamond shape.

Plate XVII. The architecture of this window is from Oxford Cathedral, which the writer has filled in with stained glass in the Gothic style.

We have here instanced a few of Walter Gedde's simple patterns. As before observed, an endless variety of figures and shapes might be introduced, and many examples of leading in ancient windows, which are still in existence, might be given. We would recommend to the reader's notice the leading

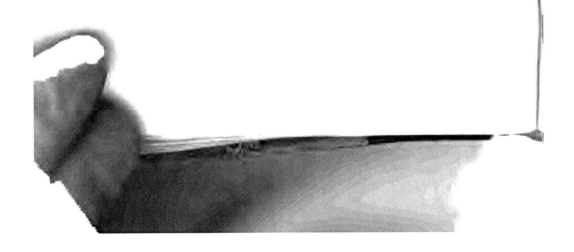

of the windows in York Minster, particularly those in the vestibule and chapter house. There are also beautiful examples of leading in the windows of Christ Church, and New College, Oxford; as well as of stained glass, executed by Jervaise, from the designs of Sir Joshua Reynolds.

The lead work can also be adapted with equal ease to any pattern that may be chosen for the glass; and it can likewise be made to any breadth, from one-eighth to five-eighths of an inch. The one-eighth, however, is only used for fancy work, and is not, as yet, much in demand; that which is most generally used, is three-eighth lead. This width makes neater and better work than that of any other dimensions.

The glazier who would include this branch of his art in his business, would do well to provide himsel with the necessary tools and apparatus for castin the lead, and act as his own plumber as well a glazier; all the knowledge of the former art whic he would require, being very easily attained. H may purchase prepared leading for windows in an quantity; but he will produce it himself at half th cost, and probably more to his own satisfaction. Tl apparatus and tools necessary for doing this, are,

glazier's vice, or lead mill, moulds for casting the
lead into slender bars or rods of about eighteen
inches in length, which is the first process; a three-
fourth inch chisel; a hard wood fillet for forcing
the glass into the grooves in the lead frame work;
and an opener or wedge tool, made also of hard
wood, or ebony, for laying open the grooves for the
reception of the glass; two copper bolts for soldering,
the end formed like an egg. Annexed are correct
drawings of the vice or mill alluded to, in describing
which, in its various connected parts, the same
letters of reference are adapted to the different
figures, so far as necessary, which, with the isometrical views, will facilitate the comprehension of
their parts and properties.

Plate XVIII. Fig. I. An end view, partly open,
of a mould for casting three varieties of patterns,
which are thus prepared for being forced through
the machine. By an ingenious construction of the
handle, it is made to lock and unlock by inclined
planes, acting on studs, *a a*. Fig. II. A side view,
also partly open; and Fig. III. an isometrical view
of the mould prepared for pouring in the metal.

The metal, or cast, being removed from the
mould, a pair of the dies, (one only of each pair is

represented,) according to the pattern required, Figs. 4, 5, 6, 7, are placed in the machine, as seen at *c c*, Fig. 8, isometrical view. After they are put in, a thin iron cover, (*b*. Fig. 10) with an oblong hole in the middle, is put on, to guide the metal into the rollers. Figs. 9, 10, and 11, represent three views of the machine as prepared for operating. In Figs. 9 and 11, the metal, *d d*, is represented passing through the machine, which is accomplished by turning the winch handle, *e e*, acting on two equal sized toothed wheels, *f f*. On the axles of these are two rollers, *g g*, slightly serrated, (dotted through in Fig. 8 and 10;) these rollers draw the metal through, while the dies give the desired form. To allow the axles and rollers to be placed in the frame, or body of the machine, A, the cover, *h*, is removed by unscrewing the bolt *i*, Figs. 8, 10, 11. The toothed wheels *f f*, are also taken off, by unscrewing the nuts *k k*. The tempering screw bolt *l*, is for adjusting the dies, after they are put in their place. The screw bolts, *m m*, are for fixing the machine to a table or bench.

Fig. 12, is an isometrical view of the cover *h* removed, to shew the ports *n n*, through which the axles of the rollers pass.

Fig. 13 shews the shape of the bolt used for sol-dering the lead windows, and Fig. 14, the opener already described.

The lead intended to be employed in window making, must be soft, and of the very best quality; and great care must be taken to have the moulds properly tempered, otherwise the lead will not be equally diffused in them, and the castings conse-quently not perfectly solid throughout, as they ought to be.

If this is not attended to, that is, if the castings are not perfectly solid, they will come out of the mill, to which they are presented, after being taken from the moulds, all fretted on the edges, and thus in a state totally unfit for the purpose for which they were intended.

The castings are, as already noticed, usually about eighteen inches in length, and are afterwards extended by the mill represented by the figure above, to the length of five or six feet.

It may not be unnecessary to add, that the mill not only extends the lead, and reduces it at the pleasure of the operator, to the dimensions required, but at the same time forms the grooves into which the edge of the glass is afterwards introduced in forming the window.

When the lead has been prepared in the manner described, the glazier ought to proceed to cut out the panes wanted. For this operation he must prepare, by drawing the shapes and sizes of the panes on a board, (and it is here understood that the intelligent glazier is capable of drawing geometrical figures correctly, when such are required,) and to these he must conform in cutting.

We will, however, perhaps be better understood, when we say that he must first outline the full dimensions of the window, and then line it off to the pattern required, shaping the panes accordingly. If the window is of a large size, this may of course be done by compartments to be afterwards united, and thus be more conveniently wrought. Great accuracy must be observed in cutting the panes, or a very irregular panel will be produced; as those lines that ought to be parallel or otherwise, will not be correctly so, which will greatly injure the appearance of the work.

When all the glass has been cut for the window, the next thing to be done, is to open the grooves in the lead with the opener or wedge tool. The panes are then, in order that they may be water tight, fastened very firmly into the grooves with the wooden fillet already spoken of, (which may be fixed on the

handle of the chisel or cutting tool,) securing the
parallel lines of lead in their proper places on the
board, when the window is of the diamond shape, by
a small nail at either end, until the course is finished,
when the work is permanently fastened by running
a small quantity of solder gently over the two con-
necting pieces of lead at each joint, or angular
point.   When the window has been completed, it
should be removed from the working board to a flat
table, where it must be covered with a thick layer
of cement, composed of white lead, lamp black, red
lead, litharge, and boiled linseed oil, with a half-
worn paint brush, and the composition carefully
rubbed into every joint.   This will render the window completely impervious to the weather, as the
cement, if properly laid on, will fill every chink,
where it will soon become as hard and durable as
any other of the materials of which the window is
composed.   When this operation has been completed, clean the window with a cloth and whiting.
Should the outside be wanted black, omit the black-
ing in the first compost; and finish by laying on the
lamp black with a polishing brush.

The window, on being fitted into the frame, that
is, on being set in its place in the building for which
it is intended, ought to be supported with three-

4

;hth inch iron rods, extending three-eighths of an
:h beyond the breadth of the frame on each side,
nning across it at the distance of from twelve to
urteen inches from each other, and secured to the
ad frame-work at intervals with copper wire or
ad bands manufactured by the mill. These rods,
'r obvious reasons, ought to be so arranged as to
itersect the window exactly at the terminating
oint of a row of the diamonds. For instance, if
he diamonds are each six inches in length or
ieight, the first rod ought to intersect the window
at the top of the third row, or eighteen inches from
the bottom of the frame, and so on, until the
window be equally divided in this way throughout
its whole length. If the diamond, again, be only
three inches in length, then the first rod ought to
pass at the top of the fourth row, or twelve inches
from the bottom, this proportion of distance being,
of course, maintained throughout. The usual
distance is fourteen inches, but this must be regulated by the breadth of the window between the
mullions. If the mullions are of stone, the groove:
in which the window is set, ought to be filled up
with Roman cement, or mastic. If of wood, with
oil putty.

Such is, in brief, the process of constructing lea

F

or lattice windows, and it is surprising that so little glazing is now done in this way. Whatever may have been the cause of its falling into desuetude, it is almost impossible to conceive that taste should have rejected an ornament at once so beautiful, and so happily combined with utility.

All who have seen specimens of ancient windows of this description, especially those filled with stained glass—and they can be as well executed at the present day as at any former period—must have felt the highest admiration of their singular beauty, elegance, and splendour. Even drawings of such windows as we allude to, forcibly impress us with a sense of their peculiar fitness for conspicuous situations, where imposing and striking effect is desired.

For churches they are peculiarly appropriate, being admirably calculated, from the solemn splendour of their character, to attune the feelings to the solemnities of devotion; and it is really singular that they are not oftener employed in this way, in cases where the character of the building would admit of it.

But it is not to churches alone that their suitableness is confined. They might be employed in many ways, either coloured or plain, with great effect, in embellishing private houses, since they form not only a highly ornamental, but a most durable and economical window.   They require no paint, nor any of that care which is necessary to protect windows, whose frames are of wood, from premature decay, and have, therefore, more than mere elegance and beauty to recommend them.

CHAPTER VI.

THE CUTTING DIAMOND.

UNDER this head, we mean to confine ourselves chiefly to a few historical and traditional notices of the diamond, and these wholly with reference to its adaptation to the purposes of the crown window glass cutter, adding a few practical remarks, partly the results of our own experience, and partly of that of others.

Before proceeding to say when diamonds were first used for cutting glass, it may not be amiss to state when the art of cutting diamonds themselves was first discovered. The ancients were ignorant of the art of cutting the diamond, and hence they used it in its natural granular or crystallized state. Though probably known to the artists of Hindostan and China at a very early period, it was unknown to the Europeans during the middle ages; for the four large diamonds which ornament the clasp of the

imperial mantle of Charlemagne, which is still pre-
served at Paris, are uncut octoedrical crystals.

In 1456, Robert de Berghen, a native of Bruges,
in the Austrian Netherlands, ' discovered that a
diamond might be cut and polished by a powder
made from itself, with the aid of certain iron wheels.
Hence the well known adage of " diamond cut
diamond."

The earliest mention of the diamond being used
for writing on glass occurs in the sixteenth century,
when the following lines, which may be considered
as the first application of the diamond to this purpose, were written by Francis the First of France
with his diamond ring on one of the panes of glass
in the Castle of Champfort. The king's purpose
in writing them was to intimate to Anne de Pisseleu,
Duchess of Estampes, that he was jealous of her:

> Souvent femme varie,
> Mal habit qui s' y fie.

> Woman is changeful as summer's sky,
> 'Tis folly to trust her constancy.

This new mode of recording ideas was then
thought exceedingly ingenious, and the merit of
having discovered a new property in the diamond
was awarded to his majesty. After this, but still

diamond was successfully employed in etching or engraving figures on glass vessels, and some very beautiful specimens of this novel art were produced at Venice as early as 1562; so that little time had been lost in applying the discovery of the French king to useful purposes.

The first noted professional engraver on glass with the diamond, of whom any thing is known, was George Schwanhard. In later times, John Rost, an artist of Augsburg, obtained great celebrity in this art. Two drinking glasses, curiously and elegantly ornamented by this artist, with his diamond pencil, were purchased by Charles VI. The art of cutting glass with a wheel, a method applicable to crystal only, was invented, in the beginning of the seventeenth century, by Caspar Lehmann, lapidary and glasscutter to the Emperor Rodolphus II.

A knowledge of the diamond, however, either for use or ornament, is not at all of remote antiquity, if we except a very few instances where it was employed, but very inefficiently, for the latter purpose. This is accounted for by the circumstance of its requiring to be cut and polished before it exhibits any degree of that shining quality which so pre-

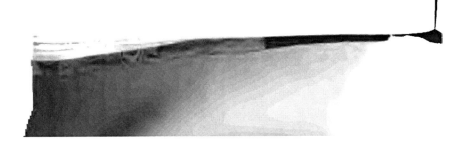

eminently distinguishes it from all other minerals.
Until, therefore, the art of cutting it was discovered,
and that is not much more than three hundred years
since, very little use could be made of it; as, in its
original rough state, it is in no way attractive, being
without lustre or beauty of colour. The ancients,
therefore, though they might be perfectly aware of
the existence of the diamond—and it is certain they
were, for mention is made of it in their writings—
must have been almost entirely ignorant of its
properties, at least we find no mention of them.
In the rare instances in which it was used by them
as an ornament, it was invariably of that description
of form which presents what is called a natural
point. This is a piece which has several natural
sides or faces, and, being transparent, is thus an
improvement on the ruder masses in which it is
generally found. It is, in short, an approximation
to artificial cutting; but the diamond is, even in
this state, without lustre, and otherwise not at all
remarkable. It is not, indeed, a century since the
full value of this precious mineral was ascertained,
and all its extraordinary properties discovered and
developed. Before its introduction as an agent in
cutting glass, that operation was performed by
means of emery, sharp pointed instruments of the

4

were the only contrivances known and practised by the ancient glaziers.

In considering the diamond in its relations to the purposes of the window-glass cutter, there occur some circumstances not unworthy of remark. Amongst these, it may be noticed, that the cutting point of the diamond must be a natural one; an artificial point, however perfectly formed, will only scratch the glass, not cut it. The diamond of a ring, for instance, will not cut a pane, but merely mark it with rough superficial lines, which penetrate but a very little way inwards. Artificial points, corners, or angles, therefore, produced by cutting the diamond are adapted only for writing or for drawing figures on glass, and such were those used by Schwanhard, Rost, and the other artists who ornamented glass vessels in the manner before alluded to. The cutting diamond does not write so well on glass, from the circumstance of its being apt to enter too deeply, and take too firm a hold of the surface, and thus become intractable. It may farther be noticed, that an accidental point, produced by fracturing the diamond, is as unfit for cutting as an artificial one. Such a point will also merely scratch the glass. No point, in short, that is not given by

he natural formation of the mineral, will answer
he purposes of the window-glass cutter.

The large sparks, as the diamonds used for cutting
glass are called, are generally preferred to the small
ones, from the circumstance of their being likely to
possess, although this is by no means invariably the
case, a number of cutting points; while the very
small sparks, for obvious reasons, are not always
found to possess more than one. Thus, if the point
of the latter is worn, or broken off, although the
spark be turned, and reset in its socket, it will still
be without the power of cutting, and consequently
useless, while the former, on undergoing the same
operation, will present a new and effective point.

The large sparks are called *mother sparks*, and
are sometimes cut down into as many smaller fragments bearing the same name, as there are natural
points in the former. Each of these, therefore, can
have only one cutting point, and are consequently
only proportionably valuable to the glazier, since
they cannot be restored by resetting.

SETTING DIAMONDS.

This is a process with which every glazier ought
to be acquainted; nor is it an art of difficult acquire-

ment; like every thing else, it requires some practice, and a little patience, but these are the only really formidable requisites it presents.

The first thing to be done is, of course, to select a stone, which must be chosen as clear and pellucid as possible, resembling a drop of water, and of an octoedrical shape, or as near to that form as possible.

Having procured such a stone, let the workman next proceed to ascertain which is its cutting point, or, if it has more than one, which is the best. This will be found to be that point which has the cutting edges of the crystal placed exactly at right angles to each other, and passing precisely through a point of intersection made by the crossing of the edges. (See Plate XIX, and explanations.)

The next thing to be done is, to provide a piece of copper or brass wire, a quarter of an inch in diameter. In one of the ends of the wire, a hole must be drilled large enough to contain three-fourths of the diamond to be set, which being temporarily secured, the setter again proceeds to ascertain the cutting point, by trying it on a piece of glass; and when he has discovered it, he must mark its position by making a slight notch in the wire with a file or otherwise, exactly opposite to the cutting point, as a guide to him in his operations,

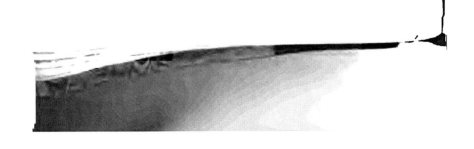

vhen he comes to fix it permanently in the socket
lead of the handle. When doing this, care must
be taken to keep it exactly parallel with the inclined
plane of the socket head.

The cutting point having been ascertained, and
the diamond fixed into its place, the wire is then
cut off about a quarter of an inch below the diamond,
and filed down to fit exactly into the aperture in the
socket head into which it must be soldered. Let
the rough or superfluous metal around the stone be
removed with a file, and finished by polishing it
with emery or sand paper. Such is the most
approved method of setting new diamonds, and it
applies equally to the resetting of old ones. But in
the latter case, the first process, that of detaching
the stone from its bed, is accomplished either by
means of a knife, or by applying the blow-pipe.

It may not be altogether superfluous to add, that
from the extremely diminutive size of the stone,
it is very apt to be lost during the operation of
setting; great care must therefore be taken to guard
against this accident. Those who are much in the
practice of setting diamonds, are provided with a
small table covered with green cloth, and surrounded
with a raised edging to catch the sparks, should
they happen to fall; but for temporary purposes,

the glass-cutter will readily fall on some expedient to secure him against an accident of this kind.

We now proceed to the explanation of the figures alluded to in another part of the article. See Plate XIX.

The annexed figures of a diamond drawn upon a large scale, are pointed agreeably to the above conditions; fig. 1 being a side and end elevation, and fig. 2, the plan of it. A B represent the leading curved part of the cutting edge of the diamond; and D, the line of intersection, crossing the line A B at right angles; E, being the following part of the cutting edge.

The general figure of the stone is farther indicated in all the figures by dotted lines. Its position in a hole formed in the metal block in which it is first adjusted, and afterwards secured as before described, is likewise shewn.

Figure 3 is a side, figure 4 a front, and figure 5 an end view of a glazier's patent diamond, mounted with a swivel adjustment, for the block F, when connected with the handle G, by means of the screw H entering into a gap filed half way through, and across the metal stem I. By this means, the cut of the diamond is much easier obtained, than when the diamond is mounted fixedly into the stem or pencil diamond.

LUKEN'S IMPROVED BEAM COMPASS FOR CUTTING CIRCLES.

This will be found a very convenient, though simple instrument, for cutting circles. Plate XIX. Fig. 6, is a perspective view or elevation of such parts of this useful instrument, as are necessary for understanding its construction, of their real size. O O is part of a square bar of brass, ten inches long, and graduated into half inches as radii, and answering to inches of the diameters of the circles, to be drawn with the instrument, and these half inches are again sub-divided into parts, and regularly numbered. Upon this bar the sliding centre, P, moves, and can be secured at any required situation by its binding screw Q. R is a cylindrical part fixed firmly upon an end of the bar; and having a conical hole made through it in a vertical direction, to receive the tapering socket of a glazier's cutting diamond, S, within it, and which can be retained in a proper direction, when the cut of the diamond is found by trial, by the binding screw T. U is a brass wire firmly fixed into the cylinder R, having its foot, V, rounded, and turned up at its end. This foot is carried evenly along, in contact with the surface of the glass to be cut, and regulates

the inclination of the diamond, as must be likewise
found by trial, and bending the wire U more or less
until the proper degree is ascertained.   The other,
or opposite side of the bar, O O, is terminated by a
brass ball affixed upon it, and the point,   P, of the
sliding centre is supported by, and turns in a small
conical hole made in a plate of metal, the back of
which is coated with a thin layer of bee's wax, which,
upon being pressed into contact with the surface of
the glass to be cut, readily adheres to it, with a
degree of firmness quite sufficient for the purpose.

The art of managing the diamond in glass-cutting,
so as to produce effective results, can only be
attained by considerable experience.   The diamond
must be held in a particular position, and with a
particular inclination, otherwise it will not cut, and
the slightest deviation from either renders an attempt
to do so abortive. In the hands of an inexperienced
person, it merely scratches the glass, leaving a long
rough furrow, but no fissure. The glazier judges by
his ear of the cut made.   When the cut is a clean
and effective one, the diamond produces, in the act
of being drawn along, a sharp, keen, and equal
sound.   When the cut is not a good one, this sound
is harsh, grating, and irregular.   On perceiving
this, the operator alters the inclination and position

of his diamond, until the proper sound is emitted, when he proceeds with his cut.

Although the diamond cuts glass of an ordinary thickness with facility, it does not so easily cut that which is of more than a medium thickness. In such cases, the desired division is effected by the application of a hot iron, which being brought in contact with the glass at certain points, produces a fissure in the direction required.

The diamonds employed in glass-cutting, are of the description known by the technical name of *bort*, a classification which includes all such pieces as are too small to be cut, or are of a bad colour, and consequently unfit for ornamental purposes. These are accordingly selected from the better sort, and sold separately, at an inferior price.

The properties of the diamond for cutting hard substances — for it is employed by seal engravers, and by engravers on copper and steel, as well as by glass-cutters — are very singular, and form, perhaps, the most remarkable feature of this remarkable mineral. The lines which it cuts on glass, in particular, when performed with a natural point, are found, even when examined by the microscope, to be exceedingly clear, smooth, and regular, and presenting such finely burnished surfaces, that, when a number of them are drawn close together, they decompose the rays of light, and exhibit the most beautiful prismatic appearances. In this there is a remarkable difference between the cuts of a natural and artificial point; for, while the former produces the effects described, the cuts made by the latter, when examined by the microscope, present exceedingly ragged edges, as if the glass was splintered into minute fragments alongst the whole line of the fissure. It may be added, also, that so delicate are the lines produced by the diamond, that two thousand of them have been drawn within the space of one inch, on plates of polished steel, which it cuts as readily as glass. It is therefore peculiarly adapted for forming the minute sub-divisions on micrometers, and other nice pieces of mechanism, for which it is often employed. Yet with the knowledge of all these facts, and a daily experience of all these effects, it is not certainly known how the diamond acts upon the glass. We know very well that it produces a cut, but, in the language of Dr Woolaston, the conditions on which the effect depends have not yet been duly investigated.

Though there are many substances that will scratch glass, the diamond was thought to be the only one that would cut it; but some experiments of Dr Woolaston have shewn that this is not strictly correct. That eminent philosopher gave to pieces of sapphire, ruby, spinel ruby, rock crystal, and some other substances, that peculiar curvilinear edge which forms the cutting point in the diamond, and in which, and in its hardness, its singular property of cutting entirely lies, and with these succeeded in cutting glass with a perfectly clear fissure. They lasted, however, but for a very short time, soon losing their edge, although prepared at a great expense of labour and care; while the diamond comes ready formed from the hand of Nature, and will last for many years.

Diamonds are found only in the East Indies, and in Brazil in South America. They are met with only in the provinces of Golconda, Visapour, Bengal, and the island of Borneo. In Clour, in Golconda, there were, at one period, no less than sixty thousand persons, men, women, and children, employed in collecting them. The finest diamonds are those that resemble a drop of pure water.

Although the history of the diamond is exceedingly curious and interesting, and a great deal has been written regarding it, we conceive that every thing has now been said which could, with any propriety, be introduced into a work of this nature.

G

CHAPTER VII.

STAINED AND PAINTED GLASS.

THE invention of the art of colouring glass—
that is, imbuing it throughout with any particular
tint—seems to be nearly coeval with the discovery
of the art of making the substance itself. Egyptian
ornaments, and Druidical beads, of the highest
antiquity, as already noticed in the historical department of this work, are found, of many and sur-
passingly beautiful colours; but the art of staining
and painting glass, so as to form pictorial represen-
tations of objects, is of comparatively recent date,
although the precise period of its introduction is
unknown. It is certain, however, that it has existed
for many centuries, but in different stages of excellence, and, like every other art, has been gradually
advancing in improvement. A pretty general, but
very erroneous, idea exists, with regard to the
superiority of the colours employed in ancient glass

ainting over those in use at the present day. It is
elieved by many, and taken for granted by others,
hat not only is the brilliancy of the former unat-
ainable by modern skill, but that the art of producing
hem is itself entirely lost. This is a very mistaken
notion, for not only are the colours now employed
as brilliant and durable as those of the ancients, but
others have been added, which they most probably
did not know how to produce, or at least did not
use. Amongst these are pink, straw colour, and
other compound tints. That indiscriminating vene-
ration for every thing ancient, which has so often,
so unjustly, and so seriously interfered with the
claims of modern merit to the encouragement to
which it is justly entitled, has operated against
glass painting and staining with perhaps fully more
force than against any other art. It has induced a
belief, that excellence in the art is confined to the
ancients — that nothing can be now done to equal
their triumphs in it—and that all the productions
of the modern glass stainer and painter are mere
flimsy imitations of those of the artists of the fourteenth and fifteenth centuries. Than this there
never was any notion more unjust or more absurd ;
and the writer feels assured, that nothing farther
is necessary to convince any one of that injustice

and absurdity, than a visit to the warehouse or workshop of any respectable glass painter and stainer of the present day.

But glass painting and staining labours under other, and perhaps greater, disadvantages than that of being reckoned a decayed art. Some of these are inherent in itself, others are contingent, and others are the result of prejudice, or spring from a deficiency of due encouragement. Not the least of these disadvantages is the circumstance of its being considered a luxury of too presumptuous a character, and of too expensive a nature, to be employed in the embellishment of the houses of persons of moderate income. This is the result of impressions derived from the uses to which painted and stained glass was of old exclusively applied,—the adornment of stupendous cathedrals, magnificent palaces, and baronial mansions — a circumstance which has had the effect of associating it with ideas of gorgeous splendour and vast expense — ideas which are yet in full operation, although the exciting cause has long since disappeared. Most people, as already remarked, are under an impression that painted or stained glass is much too expensive, and too fine a thing for them to think of indulging in as an article of luxury, and they are at no pains to correct the error, either by reflection or inquiry. Were they to make proper investigation, they would find that modern improvement has brought this elegant ornament within the reach of very moderate circumstances.

It may be remarked, too, as something singular, that while almost every other art has been called on to contribute in some way or other to our domestic comforts, or to the adornment of our dwellings, that of glass painting and staining, though its productions are not more expensive than some of these, and are certainly not inferior in elegance to many of them, should yet be but rarely applied to domestic purposes, where it could be employed with such delightful effect. When stained glass has been used in the embellishment of the mansions of the middling, or even of the upper classes, it has been hitherto in a great measure confined to hall and staircase windows, and to windows placed in similar situations, but its use might be much extended, with great advantage in point of ornamental effect.

If the windows, for instance, of a drawing-room, were filled with stained glass, whose prevailing tints should harmonize with the predominating colour in the apartment, an effect would be produced at once

novel, striking, and singularly pleasing.* Where
the expense, or any other objection, might be urged
against figured glass, in which masses of brilliant
colour are employed, that description which is plain,
and of one tint,—such as brown, ruby, pale yellow,
&c.—might be substituted; and, if selected with
reference to the prevailing colour of the interior,
with the view of either heightening or deepening its
complexion, a delightful warmth and richness of tint
would be thrown around the apartment, such as no
other contrivance of art can communicate. And
where both of these descriptions of coloured glass
might be found unsuitable—a circumstance for
which, it is apprehended, there could be only two
reasons, namely, the expense, or the too great exclu-
sion of light—there is still a third description of
ornamental glass, which might be employed, and
which is free from both of these objections. This is a
pale tracery, resembling lacework, which, when

* In connection with this part of the subject, the author has
much pleasure in recommending to the reader a very excellent
Treatise upon the Harmony of Colours by Mr Hay, painter,
Edinburgh. The work is replete with acute observation, and
displays all that exquisite taste, sound judgment, and skill, for
which Mr Hay is distinguished in his profession.

operly executed, is exceedingly beautiful, and
iparts to a room an appearance of singular light-
ess and elegance.

It would not, perhaps, be altogether accurate to
iy, that a want of taste is the cause of the neglect
rith which glass painting has been treated, and of
he very little demand that there is for it; neither
lo we think that it does entirely proceed from this
cause. It is one of those things of which it would
be, probably, more correct to say, that it has rather
been overlooked than neglected, and that, therefore,
little more is wanting than to call the public attention
to it, to procure for it a share of that popularity and
encouragement, which some more fortunate, but
certainly not more deserving arts enjoy.

Except in the name, painting on glass has no
resemblance to any other department of the pictorial
art but that of porcelain. Both the colours, and
the process of their application throughout, are
entirely different. While animal and vegetable
substances are freely used as colouring matter in
every other department of the art, they are wholly
excluded in that of glass painting, where all the
pigments used are subjected, after being laid on, to
the operation of fire, to make them penetrate the

body of the glass, or become fused on its surface —
a process which would wholly destroy the colouring
properties of such substances.   All the colours
employed in glass painting and staining are oxides
of metals or minerals, as gold, silver, cobalt, which
not only stand the fire, but require the powerful
interference of that agent to bring out their brilliancy and transparency.   Some colours, with the
application of heat, penetrate the body of the
glass, and, from this circumstance, are called
stains; while others, being mixed with a vitreous
substance called flux, become fused or vitrified on
the surface.   The former produces a variety of
colours, and all of them are perfectly transparent.
The produce of the latter are only semi-transparent, but they may be made to yield any colour or
tint required.

In preparing these colours, the most important
point to be attended to is, to have all those that are
to be used at the same time of an equal degree of
softness.   To attain this, those that are hard, and
require a great degree of heat to make them effective, must be fixed first; leaving the soft colours,
for which a slight heat only is necessary, to the
last.   If used promiscuously, and without regard to

this precaution, some of the colours would be rendered too fluid, while others would be insufficiently fused, and the work in consequence spoiled.

It is likewise of great importance to make a proper selection of glass for the purposes of staining and painting, as one kind will assimilate more freely with one colour than with another. The description of glass generally chosen for painting or staining is the best crown glass.

It is not thought advisable to enter at greater length here into the details of the process of glass painting and staining; because, in the first place, this work is intended, by the author, for the use of the glass-cutter and glazier chiefly, to whom such information is unnecessary, and which, therefore, were it introduced here, would swell the volume to too great a size. In the next place, all such details would be nearly useless for any practical purpose, there being scarcely a possibility of either communicating or acquiring such a knowledge of the art of glass painting or staining as would enable any person to practise it successfully. Nothing but personal observation and long experience can do so. And thus it is, that all the printed directions and instructions for the prosecution of the art, of which there is no lack, are found to be almost wholly useless when attempts are made to act upon them. In short, to those who have no knowledge of the art, no written instructions could be of any avail ; and to those who have, the writer has nothing new regarding it to communicate.

CHAPTER VIII.

MISCELLANEOUS.

UNDER this title we propose to throw together such desultory remarks, and odd pieces of information, as could not well be incorporated with any preceding part of this work, and which have been thought not unworthy of some place in a book compiled for the use of the glass-cutter and glazier. As these remarks and stray fragments of information, however, can neither be classified, nor reduced to any kind of regular order, they shall just be set down as they present themselves, without any attempt to give them the consistency of a narrative.

We begin with one of the most important and prominent considerations connected with the glass trade,—the window tax; and as we think every glazier should know upon what principle it proceeds, we subjoin the scheme according to which it is at present levied, remarking, that it was reduced about one-half in 1823.

DUTIES ON WINDOWS.

Number of Windows.	Duty per House per Year.	Number of Windows.	Duty per House per Year.	Number of Windows.	Duty per House per Year.	Number of Windows.	Duty per House per Year.
	L. s. d.		L. s. d.		L. s. d.		L. s. d.
8	0 15 6	22	6 8 0	35	11 17 3	80 to 84	24 6 6
9	1 0 0	23	6 16 6	36	12 5 9	85 89	25 9 0
10	1 7 0	24	7 4 9	37	12 14 3	90 94	26 11 3
11	1 15 3	25	7 13 3	38	13 2 6	95 99	27 13 9
12	2 3 9	26	8 1 9	39	13 11 0	100 109	29 7 6
13	2 12 3	27	8 10 0	40 to 44	14 7 9	110 119	31 12 3
14	3 0 9	28	8 18 6	45 49	15 15 9	120 129	33 17 3
15	3 9 0	29	9 7 0	50 54	17 4 0	130 139	36 2 0
16	3 17 6	30	9 15 3	55 59	18 12 0	140 149	38 7 0
17	4 6 0	31	10 3 9	60 64	19 16 9	150 159	40 11 9
18	4 14 3	32	10 12 3	65 69	20 19 3	160 169	42 16 9
19	5 2 9	33	11 0 6	70 74	22 1 6	170 179	45 1 6
20	5 11 3	34	11 9 0	75 79	23 4 0	180	46 10 3
21	5 19 6						

Above 180, 1s. 6d. each, in addition to £46, 10s. 3d.

EXEMPTIONS.—Farm houses occupied by a tenant at a rack-rent less than £200 per year, or in any dwelling house, being a farm house, occupied and used as aforesaid by the owner, or by any tenant of a farm or estate not at rack-rent, the value of which shall be under £100 a-year, provided he does not derive an income exceeding £100 a-year from any other source; hospitals, charity-schools, and poor-houses, (excepting the apartments for officers or servants;) places for divine worship; dairies and cheese-rooms, if " Dairy and Cheese-room" is over the door. Three windows in the shop or warehouse, if on the basement story. The windows of a room used solely for a manufactory, if not communicating with the dwelling-house.

All windows, of whatever description and wherever situated in a house, whether garrets, cellars, or staircases, and even those in outhouses, with the above exemptions, fall under this tax. Whenever the division or partition of a window amounts to or exceeds twelve inches in breadth, both sides are charged as two separate and distinct windows, and a **window,** measuring the outer aperture, exceeds welve feet in height, and four feet nine inches in breadth, it is charged as two windows. But the whole watchful ingenuity of the spirit of taxation seems to have been reserved for the following clause : — " That every window so contrived, or so situated, as to light more apartments, or other interior spaces, than one, shall be charged as so many distinct windows." Thus one window may be charged at the rate of a dozen, if it shall appear that it affords light to so many chambers, staircases, or recesses, — the purposes which it serves being taxed rather than the window itself.

The principle on which the window tax is levied, laying aside any consideration of its propriety, expediency, or equity, is not perhaps very faulty, but its operation will be found of a different character. The lower rates are too high, and the higher too low, or rather the scale descends farther down than it ought to do. The whole bearing of the tax is evidently directed, or meant to be directed, against the wealthy, or at least against those who are in comparatively easy circumstances ; but this principle cannot be recognized in the tax, when it affects such low numbers as eight, nine, ten, or even eleven and twelve windows. Besides, its progressive rise is not proportioned to what may be supposed to be the circumstances of the different individuals exposed to its operation. The person who occupies a house, or rather palace, of one hundred and eighty windows, pays only about twenty times more in the shape of window duty than he who occupies a moderate mansion of twelve; and is thus, in all probability, taxed only to the extent of about one-hundredth part of his income, while the latter, with a similar probability, pays at least one-fortieth.

But the greatest error which the tax involves, is that of its having the effect of lessening, in place of adding to the revenue. This may seem paradoxical, but it is true. It is the creating of one source of revenue at the expense of another, by taking from that other exactly the amount which it produces. This is proved by the simple circumstance of its limiting the manufacture of glass, on which a high duty is paid by the manufacturer, since it is plain, that if windows were not taxed, there would be more of them, and, as a matter of course, a greater consumption of glass. This effect of the window tax upon the revenue arising from glass, as paid by the manufacturer, is made sufficiently evident by the fact, that, for the three years ending 1828, the increase in the home consumption of window glass, over that of the three years ending with 1791, was only two per cent, although the number of buildings in many towns and cities in Great Britain has, in that time, been in some cases nearly, and in others more than doubled, as appears from the increase on bricks and tiles during the same period, an increase amounting to ninety per cent.

But the evils of the window tax are not yet exhausted. It is in the last degree prejudicial to a valuable branch of the national trade, — the glass trade, and, of consequence, to all the various interests connected with it, some of which are of vital importance to the state itself, particularly that of shipping, and the manufacture of kelp, the latter of which involves not only the comfort, but the very existence of thousands of the indigent inhabitants of the Orkneys, and Western Isles, and main land of Scotland.

The window tax has the most prejudicial effects on our domestic architecture. One of these has been the introduction of a mode of building, by which the size and number of windows have been diminished, at the expense of taste, symmetry, elegance, comfort, and even health. Surely a tax, which is attended with such prejudicial consequences as this, ought to be abolished, the more especially when it is considered, that such abolition would not be followed by any diminution of revenue, since, as has been already shewn, a proportional increase would undoubtedly take place in the duties levied on the manufacturers.

It will not have escaped the reader, amongst other considerations which this discussion will have suggested, that glass is more unfortunately situated than any other subject of taxation, inasmuch as it is not *once* taxed, like other things, but *twice*,—first as glass, and again as a window.

How this unoffending and most useful article should have provoked such an extraordinary measure of persecution, we believe no one can explain. Considering the present state of our national finances, we do not pretend to assert, that the duty on window glass should be taken off; but the window tax, for reasons already named, ought in justice to be abolished. It is so apt to be considered under the obnoxious aspect of being a tax on the light of heaven, and the vital air, that it were well if some adequate, and less generally objectionable substitute for it could be discovered by the legislature. As it is, it must be allowed to the best specimens of the art of imposing

2

:es, which even this land, so celebrated for its
cation, can exhibit.

DUTIES, DRAWBACKS, &c.

The first duties granted on glass, were imposed
r Statute 6 and 7, of William III. These duties
ere ordained by a subsequent Act to be perma-
ent, but were afterwards taken off. By Statute 19,
Geo. II. c. 12, an excise duty is laid upon glass
f 8d. per lb. upon all crown, plate, and flint glass
imported. Other and higher duties were imposed
by subsequent Acts. The duty now levied on
crown glass, is 73s. 6d. per cwt. A drawback to
the same amount is allowed on crown glass in tables
or half tables, exported from Great Britain and
Ireland; and on crown glass cut into panes, none
less than 6×4 inches, 98s. per cwt. except in the
cases of exportation to the isle of Wight, Jersey,
Guernsey, Alderney, and Man, when the drawback
is 73s. 6d. per cwt. on tables or half tables, and
no drawback on panes. No drawback is allowed
upon yolks or bullions, when exported. It may be
worth while to remark, that though a greater allowance is made upon squares than sheets, when
exported, there is little advantage in cutting up
glass for a foreign market, since the bullion and

H

waste in cutting, on which no drawback is allowed in any case, is just about equal to the difference.

Crown-glass must be entered and shipped within twelve months after being packed and sealed; but the commissioners of excise may permit glass to be repacked, provided the invoice duty has been paid on the article within the last three years.

To those who import their glass coast-ways, it may be of some consequence to know, that a barrel bulk, the standard by which the freight of port dues of crates, and almost all other things brought by sea is charged, is five cubic feet, and that a twelve table crate is about three barrel bulk. Let the purchaser look to this, when settling his freight accounts.

The duties levied on crown glass and foreign timber, are returned to the heritors or builders of churches, belonging to the establishments in England, Scotland, and Ireland. The form for obtaining this drawback of duty on crown glass, is to get the measurements of the glass used, attested by the excise officer and supervisor of the district. The heritors also give attestation as to the purposes to which the glass has been applied; and the manufacturer of the glass attaches his affidavit of having paid the duty. This document is forwarded to the oard of Excise, London, who transmit orders to the collector of the district for payment, at the rate of 73s. 6d. per cwt.

In our account of the manufacture, we omitted to mention, that the use of kelp in the manufacture of glass, is now generally declining. Of late, the improvements in the manufacture of carbonate of soda have been very great, while it has also fallen considerably in price. Instead, therefore, of using such an impure alkali as kelp with sand, pure carbonate of soda with sand and lime are now employed. These materials produce glass of as good a colour as plate, besides possessing many other advantages over the old ingredients. The preparation of the carbonate of soda for this purpose, is carried on within their own premises, by some of the most extensive manufacturers.

CHAPTER IX.

MEASUREMENT OF GLASS.

To shew the contents of any given number of panes would occupy a volume of itself. The following instructions and Tables, are all that are necessary for the glazier's use :

No. I. shews the contents of panes from 10 in. $\times$ 7 in. to 28 in. $\times$ 20 in., increasing by 1 inch each way.

			in.	in.	in.	in.
II.	.	.	$10\frac{1}{4} \times 7$	to	$28\frac{1}{4} \times 20$	
III.	.	.	$10\frac{1}{4} \times 7\frac{1}{4}$	to	$28\frac{1}{4} \times 20\frac{1}{4}$	
IV.	.	.	$10\frac{1}{2} \times 7$	to	$28\frac{1}{2} \times 20$	
V.	.	.	$10\frac{1}{2} \times 7\frac{1}{2}$	to	$28\frac{1}{2} \times 20\frac{1}{2}$	
VI.	.	.	$10\frac{3}{4} \times 7$	to	$28\frac{3}{4} \times 20$	
VII.	.	.	$10\frac{3}{4} \times 7\frac{3}{4}$	to	$28\frac{3}{4} \times 20\frac{3}{4}$	
VIII.	.	.	4×3	to	$9\frac{1}{2} \times 6\frac{1}{2}$	

To find the contents of any given square,—say
$24\frac{1}{4}$ inches $\times$ 14 inches.

In page 120, Table No. II. look for the length $24\frac{1}{4}$, and on the angular line for the width 14 ; in the same column, and opposite to $24\frac{1}{4}$, you have 28

nches and three parts, or 399 square inches = 2 sq.
t. 51 sq. in.—Contents of the square of glass, 24¼
in. × 14 in.

Fractional parts of an inch for finding the contents
in square measure.

	pts. or 2ds.	3ds.
⅛ inch =	1″	6‴
¼ do. =	3	
⅜ do. =	4	6
½ do. =	6	
⅝ do. =	7	6
¾ do. =	9	
⅞ do. =	10	6

12 fourths = 1 third.
12 thirds = 1 part or second.
12 seconds = 1 inch.
12 inches = 1 foot.

RULE.

To find the contents of a pane of glass.

I. Place feet under feet, inches under inches,
seconds under seconds, &c.

II. Multiply each denomination of the length by
the feet of the breadth, beginning at the lowest, and
place each product directly under the corresponding
denomination from which it arises, and carry one
for every 12.

III. Multiply by the inches, and set each product one place farther to the right hand, then multiply by the parts or seconds, and set each product another place farther toward the right hand.

IV. Proceed in the same manner with all the rest of the denominations, namely, 3ds, 4ths, &c., and their sum will be the contents.

NOTE.

Feet   × by feet give feet.
Feet   × by inches give inches.
Feet   × by seconds give seconds or parts.
Inches   × by inches give seconds.
Inches   × by seconds give thirds.
Inches   × by thirds give fourths.
Seconds × by seconds give fourths.
Seconds × by thirds give fifths.
Seconds × by fourths give sixths.
Thirds   × by thirds give sixths.
&c.   &c.

in.		in.	pts.	3ds.	4ths.	5ths.
$\frac{1}{8}$	×	$\frac{1}{8}$ =	0	0	2	3
$\frac{3}{8}$	×	$\frac{3}{8}$ =	0	1	8	3
$\frac{5}{8}$	×	$\frac{5}{8}$ =	0	4	8	3
$\frac{7}{8}$	×	$\frac{7}{8}$ =	0	9	2	3

Ex. 1st. $14\frac{1}{8}$ in. × $12\frac{1}{8}$ in.   2d. $14\frac{3}{8}$ in. × $12\frac{3}{8}$ in.

ft.	in.	2ds.	3ds.				ft.	in.	pts.	3ds.
1	2	1	6				1	2	4	6
1	0	1	6				1	0	4	6
1	2	1	6				1	2	4	6
	1	2	1	6				4	9	6
		7	0	9					7	2	3
1	2	3	3	2	3		1	2	9	10	8	3

3d.   14¼ in. × 12¼ in.

ft.	in.	2ds.	3ds.
1	2	3	
1	0	3	
---	---	---	---
1	2	3	
		3	6	9
---	---	---	---
1	2	6	6	9

4th.   14⅓ in. × 12⅓ in.

ft.	in.	pts.	3ds.
1	2	6	
1	0	6	
---	---	---	---
1	2	6,	
		7	3
---	---	---	---
1	3	1	3

5th.   14⅝ in. × 13⅝ in.

ft.	in.	pts.	3ds.		
1	2	7	6		
1	1	7	6		
---	---	---	---	---	---
1	2	7	6		
	1	2	7	6	
	8	6	4	6	
		7	3	9	
---	---	---	---	---	---
1	4	7	3	2	3

6th.   14¾ in. × 13¾ in.

ft.	in.	pts.		
1	2	9		
1	1	9		
---	---	---	---	---
1	2	9		
	1	2	9	
		11	0	9
---	---	---	---	---
1	4	10	9	9

7th.   14⅞ in. × 13⅞ in.

ft.	in.	2ds.	3ds.		
1	2	10	6		
1	1	10	6		
---	---	---	---	---	---
1	2	10	6		
	1	2	10	6	
	1	0	4	9	
			7	5	3
---	---	---	---	---	---
1	5	2	4	8	3

Note.—The feet in the product are square feet, and the inches are twelfth parts of a square foot, or each of them is equal to twelve square inches, and the parts are square inches. The lower denominations are generally expressed in fractions of a square inch; thus, 4 parts are ⅓ of a square inch, 10 parts are $\frac{5}{6}$, &c.

The following Tables are expressed in *Duodecimal Inches and Parts*; and may, if necessary, be easily converted into square inches, by multiplying the inches by 12, and adding the parts to the product.

INCHES BROAD.

INCHES LONG.

IN.	7	8	9	10	11	12	13	14	15	16	17	18	19	20
	L. P.	L. P.	L. P.	L. P.	L. P.	L. P.	L. P.	L. P.	L. P.	L. P.	L. P.	L. P.	L. P.	L. P.
10	5.10	6.8	7.6	8.4										
11	6.5	7.4	8.3	9.2	10.1									
12	7.0	8.0	9.0	10.0	11.0	12.0								
13	7.7	8.8	9.9	10.10	11.11	13.0	14.1							
14	8.2	9.4	10.6	11.8	12.10	14.0	15.2	16.4						
15	8.9	10.0	11.3	12.6	13.9	15.0	16.3	17.6	18.9					
16	9.4	10.8	12.0	13.4	14.8	16.0	17.4	18.8	20.0	21.4				
17	9.11	11.4	12.9	14.2	15.7	17.0	18.5	19.10	21.3	22.8	24.1			
18	10.6	12.0	13.6	15.0	16.6	18.0	19.6	21.0	22.6	24.0	25.6	27.0		
19	..	..	..	..	17.5	19.0	20.7	22.2	23.9	25.4	26.11	28.6	30.1	
20	..	..	..	..	18.4	20.0	21.8	23.4	25.0	26.8	28.4	30.0	31.8	
21	..	..	..	..	19.3	21.0	22.9	24.6	26.3	28.0	29.9	31.6	33.3	
22	..	..	..	..	20.2	22.0	23.10	25.8	27.6	29.4	31.2	33.0	34.10	
23	..	..	..	..	21.1	23.0	24.11	26.10	28.9	30.8	32.7	34.6	36.5	
24	..	..	..	..	22.0	24.0	26.0	28.0	30.0	32.0	34.0	36.0	38.0	
25	..	..	..	..	22.11	25.0	27.1	29.2	31.3	33.4	35.5	37.6	39.7	
26	..	..	..	..	23.10	26.0	28.2	30.4	32.6	34.8	36.10	39.0	41.2	
27	..	..	..	..	24.9	27.0	29.3	31.6	33.9	36.0	38.3	40.6	42.9	
28	..	..	..	..	25.8	28.0	30.4	32.8	35.0	37.4	39.8	42.0	44.4	

No. I.   From 10 in.✕7 in. to 28 in. by 20 in.

INCHES BROAD.

INCHES LONG.

IN.	7	8	9	10	11	12	13	14	15	16	17	18	19	20
	L. P.	L. P.	L. P.	L. P.	L. P.	L. P.	L. P.	L. P.	L. P.	L. P.	L. P.	L. P.	L. P.	L. P.
10¼	5.11	6.10	7.8	8.6										
11¼	6.6	7.6	8.5	9.4	10.3									
12¼	7.1	8.2	9.2	10.3	11.2	12.3								
13¼	7.8	8.10	9.11	11.0	12.1	13.2	14.4							
14¼	8.3	9.6	10.8	11.10	13.0	14.3	15.5	16.7						
15¼	8.10	10.2	11.5	12.8	13.11	15.3	16.6	17.9	19.0					
16¼	9.5	10.10	12.2	13.6	14.10	16.3	17.7	18.11	20.3	21.9				
17¼	10.0	11.6	12.11	14.4	15.9	17.3	18.8	20.1	21.6	23.0	24.5			
18¼	10.7	12.2	13.8	15.2	16.8	18.3	19.9	21.3	22.9	24.4	25.10	27.4		
19¼	11.2	12.10	14.5	16.0	17.7	19.3	20.10	22.5	24.0	25.8	27.3	28.10	30.5	
20¼	11.9	13.6	15.2	16.10	18.6	20.3	21.11	23.7	25.3	27.0	28.0	30.4	32.0	
21¼	..	..	..	..	19.6	21.3	23.0	24.9	26.6	28.4	30.1	31.10	33.7	
22¼	..	..	..	..	20.4	22.3	24.1	25.11	27.9	29.8	31.6	33.4	35.2	
23¼	..	..	..	..	21.3	23.3	25.2	27.1	29.0	31.0	32.11	34.10	36.9	
24¼	..	..	..	..	22.2	24.3	26.3	28.3	30.3	32.4	34.4	36.4	38.4	
25¼	..	..	..	..	23.1	25.3	27.4	29.5	31.6	33.8	35.9	37.10	39.11	
26¼	..	..	..	..	24.0	26.3	28.5	30.7	32.9	35.0	37.2	39.4	41.0	
27¼	..	..	..	..	24.11	27.3	29.6	31.9	34.0	36.6	38.7	40.10	43.1	
28¼	..	..	..	..	25.10	28.3	30.7	32.11	35.3	37.8	40.0	42.4	44.8	

No. II.   From 10¼ in.✕7 in. to 28¼ in.✕20 in.

INCHES BROAD.

IN	7¼	8¼	9¼	10¼	11¼	12¼	13¼	4¼	15¼	16¼	17¼	18¼	19¼	20¼
	I. P.	I. P.	I. P.	I. P.										
10¼	6.2	7.0	7.10	8.9	I. P.									
11¼	6.9	7.8	8.8	9.7	10.6	I. P.								
12¼	7.4	8.5	9.5	10.5	11.5	12.6	I. P.							
13¼	8.0	9.1	10.2	11.3	12.5	13.6	14.7	I. P.						
14¼	8.7	9.9	10.11	12.2	13.4	14.6	15.8	16.11	I. P.					
15¼	9.2	10.6	11.9	13.0	14.3	15.6	16.10	18.1	19.4	I. P.				
16¼	9.9	11.2	12.6	13.10	15.2	16.7	17.11	19.3	20.8	22.0	I. P.			
17¼	10.5	11.9	13.3	14.8	16.2	17.7	19.0	20.5	21.11	23.4	24.9	I. P.		
18¼	11.0	12.6	14.0	15.7	17.1	18.7	20.1	21.8	23.2	24.8	26.3	27.9	I. P.	
19¼	11.7	13.2	14.10	16.5	18.0	19.7	21.3	22.10	24.5	26.1	27.8	29.3	30.10	I. P.
20¼	12.2	13.11	15.7	17.3	18.11	20.8	22.4	24.0	25.8	27.5	29.1	30.9	32.6	34.2
21¼	. .	. .	. .	. .	19.11	21.8	23.5	25.2	27.0	28.9	30.6	32.3	34.1	35.10
22¼	. .	. .	. .	. .	20.10	22.8	24.6	26.5	28.3	30.1	31.11	33.10	35.8	37.6
23¼	. .	. .	. .	. .	21.8	23.8	25.8	27.7	29.7	31.5	33.5	35.4	37.3	39.2
24¼	. .	. .	. .	. .	22.9	24.9	26.9	28.9	30.9	32.10	34.10	36.10	38.10	40.11
25¼	. .	. .	. .	. .	23.8	25.9	27.10	29.11	32.1	34.2	36.3	38.4	40.6	42.7
26¼	. .	. .	. .	. .	24.7	26.9	28.11	31.2	33.4	35.6	37.8	39.11	42.1	44.3
27¼	. .	. .	. .	. .	25.6	27.9	30.1	32.4	34.7	36.10	39.2	41.5	43.8	45.11
28¼	.	. .	. .	. .	26.5	28.10	31.2	33.5	35.10	38.3	40.7	42.11	45.3	47.8

No. III. From 10¼ in. × 7¼ in., to 28¼ in. × 20¼ in.

INCHES BROAD.

IN.	7	8	9	10	11	12	13	14	15	16	17	18	19	20
	I. P.	I. P.	I. P.	I. P.										
10½	6.1	7.0	7.10	8.9	I. P.									
11½	6.8	7.8	8.7	9.7	10.6	I. P.								
12½	7.3	8.4	9.4	10.[illegible]	11.5	12.6	I. P.							
13½	7.10	9.0	10.1	1[illegible].3	12.4	13.6	14.7	I. P.						
14½	8.5	9.8	10.10	12.1	13.3	14.6	15.8	16.11	I. P.					
15½	9.0	10.4	11.7	12.11	14.2	15.6	16.9	18.1	19.4	I. P.				
16½	9.7	11.0	12.4	13.9	15.1	16.6	17.10	19.3	20.7	22.0	I. P.			
17½	10.2	11.8	13.1	14.7	16.0	17.6	18.11	20.5	21.10	23.4	24.9	I. P.		
18½	10.9	12.4	13.10	15.5	16.11	18.6	20.0	21.7	23.1	24.8	26.2	27.9	I. P.	
19½	11.4	13.0	14.7	16.3	17.10	19.6	21.1	22.9	24.4	26.0	27.7	29.3	30.10	I. P.
20½	11.11	13.0	15.4	17.1	18.9	20.6	22.2	23.11	25.7	27.4	29.0	30.9	32.5	34.2
21½	. .	. .	. .	. .	19.8	21.6	23.3	25.1	26.10	28.8	30.5	32.3	34.0	35.10
22½	. .	. .	. .	. .	20.7	22.6	24.4	26.3	28.1	30.0	31.10	33.9	35.7	37.6
23½	. .	. .	. .	. .	21.7	23.6	25.5	27.5	29.4	31.4	33.3	35.3	37.2	39.2
24½	. .	. .	. .	. .	22.5	24.6	26.6	28.7	30.7	32.8	34.8	36.9	38.9	40.10
25½	. .	. .	. .	. .	23.4	25.6	27.7	29.9	31.10	34.0	36.1	38.3	40.4	42.6
26½	. .	. .	. .	. .	24.3	26.6	28.8	30.11	33.1	35.4	37.6	39.9	41.11	44.2
27½	. .	. .	. .	. .	25.2	27.6	29.9	32.1	34.4	36.8	38.11	41.3	43.6	45.10
28½	. .	. .	. .	. .	26.1	28.6	30.10	33.3	35.7	38.0	40.4	42.9	45.1	47.6

INCHES LONG.

No. IV. From 10½ in. × 7 in. to 28½ in. × 20 in.

INCHES BROAD.

IN.	7½	8½	9½	10½	11½	12½	13½	14½	15½	16½	17½	18½	19½	20½
	I. P.	I. P.	I. P.	I. P.	I. P.	I. P.	I. P.	I. P.	I. P.	I. P.	I. P.	I. P.	I. P.	I. P.
10½	6.6	7.5	8.3	9.2										
11½	7.2	8.1	9.1	10.0	11.0									
12½	7.9	8.10	9.10	10.11	11.11	13.0								
13½	8.5	9.6	10.8	11.9	12.11	14.0	15.2							
14½	9.0	10.3	11.5	12.8	13.10	15.1	16.3	17.6						
15½	9.8	10.11	12.3	13.6	14.10	16.1	17.5	18.8	20.0					
16½	10.3	11.8	13.0	14.5	15.9	17.2	18.6	19.11	21.3	22.8				
17½	10.11	12.4	13.10	15.3	16.9	18.2	19.8	21.1	22.7	24.0	25.6			
18½	11.6	13.1	14.7	16.2	17.8	19.3	20.9	22.4	23.10	25.5	26.11	28.6		
19½	12.2	13.9	15.5	17.0	18.8	20.3	21.11	23.6	25.2	26.9	28.5	30.0	31.8	
20½	12.9	14.6	16.2	17.11	19.7	21.4	23.0	24.9	26.5	28.2	29.10	31.7	33.3	
21½	..	..	..	..	20.7	22.4	24.2	25.11	27.9	29.6	31.4	33.1	34.11	
22½	..	..	..	..	21.6	23.5	25.3	27.2	29.0	30.11	32.9	34.8	36.6	
23½	..	..	..	..	22.6	24.5	26.5	28.4	30.4	32.3	34.3	36.2	38.2	
24½	..	..	..	..	23.5	25.6	27.6	29.7	31.7	33.8	35.8	37.9	39.9	
25½	..	..	..	..	24.5	26.6	28.8	30.9	32.11	35.0	37.2	39.3	41.5	
26½	..	..	..	..	25.4	27.7	29.9	32.0	34.2	36.5	38.7	40.10	43.0	
27½	..	..	..	..	26.4	28.7	30.11	33.2	35.6	37.9	40.1	42.4	44.8	
28½	..	..	..	..	27.3	29.8	32.0	34.5	36.9	39.2	41.6	43.11	46.3	

No. V. From 10½ in.×7½ in. to 28½ in.×20½ in.

INCHES BROAD.

IN.	7	8	9	10	11	12	13	14	15	16	17	18	19	20
	I. P.	I. P.	I. P.	I. P.	I. P.	I. P.	I. P.	I. P.	I. P.	I. P.	I. P.	I. P.	I. P.	I. P.
10¾	6.3	7.2	8.0	8.11										
11¾	6.10	7.10	8.9	9.9	10.9									
12¾	7.5	8.6	9.6	10.7	11.8	12.9								
13¾	8.0	9.2	10.3	11.5	12.7	13.9	14.10							
14¾	8.7	9.10	11.0	12.3	13.6	14.9	15.11	17.2						
15¾	9.2	10.6	11.9	13.1	14.5	15.9	17.0	18.4	19.8					
16¾	9.9	11.2	12.6	13.11	15.4	16.9	18.1	19.6	20.11	22.4				
17¾	10.4	11.10	13.3	14.9	16.3	17.9	19.2	20.8	22.2	23.8	25.1			
18¾	10.11	12.6	14.0	15.7	17.2	18.9	20.3	21.10	23.5	25.0	26.6	28.1		
19¾	11.6	13.2	14.9	16.5	18.1	19.9	21.4	23.0	24.11	26.4	27.11	29.7	31.3	
20¾	12.1	13.10	15.6	17.3	19.0	20.9	22.5	24.2	25.11	27.8	29.4	31.1	32.10	34.7
21¾	..	..	..	..	19.11	21.9	23.6	25.4	27.2	29.0	30.9	32.7	34.5	36.3
22¾	..	..	..	..	20.10	22.9	24.7	26.6	28.5	30.4	32.2	34.1	36.0	37.11
23¾	..	..	..	..	21.9	23.9	25.8	27.8	29.8	31.8	33.7	35.7	37.7	39.7
24¾	..	..	..	..	22.7	24.9	26.9	28.10	30.11	33.0	35.0	37.1	39.2	41.3
25¾	..	..	..	..	23.7	25.9	27.10	30.0	32.2	34.4	36.5	38.7	40.9	42.11
26¾	..	..	..	..	24.6	26.9	28.11	31.2	33.5	35.8	37.10	40.1	42.4	44.7
27¾	..	..	..	..	25.5	27.9	30.0	32.4	34.8	37.0	39.3	41.7	43.11	46.3
28¾	..	..	..	..	26.4	28.9	31.1	33.6	35.11	38.4	40.8	43.1	45.6	47.11

No. VI. From 10¾ in.×7 in. to 28¾ in.×20 in.

INCHES BROAD.

In.	7¾	8¾	9¾	10¾	11¾	12¾	13¾	14¾	15¾	16¾	17¾	18¾	19¾	20¾
IN.	I. P.	I. P.	I. P.	I. P.	I. P.	I. P.	I. P.	I. P.	I. P.	I. P.	I. P.	I. P.	I. P.	I. P.
10¾	6.11	7.10	8.8	9.7										
11¾	7.7	8.6	9.6	10.6	11.6									
12¾	8.2	9.3	10.4	11.5	12.5	13.6								
13¾	8.10	10.0	11.2	12.3	13.5	14.7	15.9							
14¾	9.6	10.9	11.11	13.2	14.5	15.8	16.10	18.1						
15¾	10.2	11.5	12.9	14.1	15.5	16.8	18.0	19.4	20.8					
16¾	10.9	12.2	13.7	15.0	16.4	17.9	19.2	20.7	21.11	23.4				
17¾	11.5	12.10	14.5	15.10	17.4	18.10	20.4	21.9	23.3	24.9	26.3			
18¾	12.1	13.8	15.2	16.9	18.4	19.11	21.5	23.0	24.7	26.2	27.8	29.3		
19¾	12.9	14.3	16.0	17.8	19.4	20.11	22.7	24.3	25.11	27.6	29.2	30.10	32.6	
20¾	13.4	15.1	16.10	18.6	20.3	22.0	23.9	25.6	27.3	28.11	30.8	32.5	34.2	35.10
21¾	..	..	..	..	21.3	23.1	24.11	26.8	28.6	30.4	32.2	33.11	35.9	37.7
22¾	..	..	..	..	22.3	24.2	26.0	27.11	29.10	31.9	33.7	35.6	37.5	39.4
23¾	..	..	..	..	23.3	25.2	27.2	29.2	31.2	33.1	35.1	37.1	39.1	41.0
24¾	..	..	..	..	24.0	26.4	28.4	30.5	32.5	34.6	36.7	38.8	40.8	42.9
25¾	..	..	..	..	25.0	27.4	29.6	31.7	33.9	35.11	38.1	40.2	42.4	44.6
26¾	..	..	..	..	26.2	28.5	30.7	32.10	35.1	37.4	39.6	41.9	44.0	46.3
27¾	..	..	..	..	27.2	29.5	31.9	34.1	36.5	38.8	41.0	43.4	45.8	47.3
28¾	..	..	..	..	28.1	30.6	32.11	35.4	37.8	40.1	42.6	44.11	47.3	49.8

INCHES LONG.

No. VII. From 10¾ in. × 7¾ in. to 28¾ in. × 20¾ in.

INCHES BROAD.

3	3½	4	4½	5	5½	6	6½	In.
I. P.	I. P.	I. P.	I. P.	I. P.	I. P.	I. P.	I. P.	In.
1.0	1.2	1.4	1.6	1.8	1.10	2.0	2.2	4
1.2	1.4	1.6	1.8	1.11	2.1	2.3	2.5	4½
1.3	1.6	1.8	1.11	2.1	2.4	2.6	2.9	5
1.5	1.7	1.10	2.1	2.4	2.6	2.9	3.0	5½
1.6	1.9	2.0	2.3	2.6	2.9	3.0	3.3	6
	1.11	2.2	2.5	2.9	3.0	3.3	3.6	6½
		2.4	2.7	2.11	3.3	3.6	3.10	7
			2.9	3.2	3.5	3.9	4.1	7½
				3.4	3.8	4.0	4.4	8
					3.11	4.3	4.7	8½
						4.6	4.11	9
							5.3	9½

INCHES LONG.

No. VIII. Small or box sizes, from 4 in. × 3 in. to 9½ in. × 6½ in.

TABLE SHEWING THE VALUE OF ANY SQUARE OF GLASS FROM FIVE TO FORTY-EIGHT INCHES, AT VARIOUS PRICES.

Squares containing	Inches.	@ 1/3 ⅌ foot		@ 1/4 ⅌ foot		@ 1/5 ⅌ foot		@ 1/6 ⅌ foot		@ 1/9 ⅌ foot		@ 2/ ⅌ foot		@ 2/3 ⅌ foot		@ 2/6 ⅌ foot		@ 2/9 ⅌ foot		@ 3/ ⅌ foot	
		s.	d.	s.	d.	s.	d.	s.	d.	s.	d.	s.	d.	s.	d.	s.	d.	s.	d.	s.	d.
	5	0	6¼	0	6⅔	0	7	0	7½	0	8¾	0	10	0	11¼	1	0½	1	1¾	1	3
	6	0	0	0	8	0	8½	0	9	0	10½	1	0	1	1½	1	3	1	4½	1	6
	7	0	8¾	0	9⅓	0	9¾	0	10½	1	0¼	1	2	1	3¾	1	5½	1	7¼	1	9
	8	0	10	0	10⅔	0	11⅓	1	0	1	2	1	4	1	6	1	8	1	10	2	0
	9	0	11¼	1	0	1	0¾	1	1½	1	3¾	1	6	1	8¼	1	10½	2	0¾	2	3
	10	1	0½	1	1⅓	1	2	1	3	1	5½	1	8	1	10½	2	1	2	3½	2	6
	11	1	1¾	1	2⅔	1	3½	1	4½	1	7¼	1	10	2	0¾	2	3½	2	6¼	2	9
1 Foot or	12	1	3	1	4	1	5	1	6	1	9	2	0	2	3	2	6	2	9	3	0
	13	1	4¼	1	5⅓	1	6½	1	7½	1	10¾	2	2	2	5¼	2	8½	2	11¾	3	3
	14	1	5½	1	6⅔	1	7¾	1	9	2	0½	2	4	2	7½	2	11	3	2½	3	6
	15	1	6¾	1	8	1	9¼	1	10½	2	2¼	2	6	2	9¾	3	1½	3	5¼	3	9
	16	1	8	1	9⅓	1	10⅔	2	0	2	4	2	8	3	0	3	4	3	8	4	0
	17	1	9¼	1	10⅔	2	0	2	1½	2	5¾	2	10	3	2¼	3	6½	3	10¾	4	3
1½ Feet or	18	1	10½	2	0	2	1½	2	3	2	7½	3	0	3	4½	3	9	4	1½	4	6
	19	1	11¾	2	1⅓	2	3	2	4½	2	9¼	3	2	3	6¾	3	11½	4	4¼	4	9
	20	2	1	2	2⅔	2	4⅓	2	6	2	11	3	4	3	9	4	2	4	7	5	0
	21	2	2¼	2	4	2	5¾	2	7½	3	0¾	3	6	3	11¼	4	4½	4	9¾	5	3
	22	2	3½	2	5⅓	2	7	2	9	3	2½	3	8	4	1½	4	7	5	0½	5	6
	23	2	4¾	2	6⅔	2	8½	2	10½	3	4¼	3	10	4	3¾	4	9½	5	3¼	5	9
2 Feet or	24	—		2	8	2	10	3	0	3	6	4	0	4	6	5	0	5	6	6	0
	25	—		2	9⅓	2	11½	3	1½	3	7¾	4	2	4	8¼	5	2½	5	8¾	6	3
	26	—		2	10⅔	3	0¾	3	3	3	9½	4	4	4	10½	5	5	5	11½	6	6
	27	—		3	0	3	2¼	3	4½	3	11¼	4	6	5	0¾	5	7½	6	2¼	6	9
	28	—		3	1	3	3⅔	3	6	4	1	4	8	5	3	5	10	6	5	7	0
	29	—		3	2⅔	3	5	3	7½	4	2¾	4	10	5	5¼	6	0½	6	7¾	7	3
	30	—		3	4	3	6½	3	9	4	4½	5	0	5	7½	6	3	6	10½	7	6
	31	—		3	5⅓	3	7¾	3	10½	4	6¼	5	2	5	9¾	6	5½	7	1¼	7	9
	32	—		3	6⅔	3	9⅓	4	0	4	8	5	4	6	0	6	8	[illegible]	[illegible]	8	0
	33	—		3	8	3	10¾	4	1½	4	9¾	5	6	6	2¼	6	10½	7	6¾	8	3
	34	—		3	9	4	0	4	3	4	11½	5	8	6	4½	7	1	7	9½	8	6
	35	—		3	10⅔	4	1½	4	4½	5	1¼	5	10	6	6¾	7	3½	8	0¼	8	9
3 Feet or	36	—		—		4	3	4	6	5	3	6	0	6	9	7	6	8	3	9	0
	37	—		—		4	4½	4	7½	5	4¾	6	2	6	11¼	7	8½	8	5¾	9	3
	38	—		—		4	5¾	4	9	5	6½	6	4	7	1½	7	11	8	8½	9	6
	39	—		—		4	7¼	4	10½	5	8¼	6	6	7	[illegible]	8	1½	8	11¼	9	9
	40	—		—		4	8⅔	5	0	5	10	6	8	7	6	8	4	9	2	10	0
	41	—		—		4	10	5	1½	5	11¾	6	10	7	8¼	8	6½	9	4¾	10	3
	42	—		—		4	11½	5	3	6	1½	7	0	7	10½	8	9	9	7½	10	6
	43	—		—		5	0¾	5	4½	6	3¼	7	2	8	0¾	8	11½	9	10¼	10	9
	44	—		—		5	2	5	6	6	5	7	4	8	3	9	2	10	1	11	0
	45	—		—		5	3¾	5	7½	6	6¾	7	6	8	5¼	9	4½	10	3¾	11	3
	46	—		—		5	5	5	9	6	8½	7	8	8	7½	9	7	10	6½	11	6
	47	—		—		5	6½	5	10½	6	10¼	7	10	8	9¾	9	9½	10	9¼	11	9
4 Feet or	48	—		—		5	8	6	0	7	0	8	0	9	0	10	0	11	0	12	0
3 parts or ¼ in.		—		—		0	0⅓	0	0⅜	0	0½	0	0½	0	0½	0	0⅝	0	0¾	0	0¾
6 parts or ½ in.		—		—		0	0¾	0	0¾	0	0¾	0	1	0	1⅛	0	1¼	0	1⅜	0	1½
9 parts or ¾ in.		—		—		0	1	0	1⅛	0	1¼	0	1½	0	1¾	0	2	0	2⅛	0	2¼

Square containing	Inches.	@ foot	@ foot	@ foot	@ foot	@ foot	@ foot	@ foot	@ foot	@ foot	@ foot
		s. d.	s. d.	s. d.	s. d.	s. d.	s. d.	s. d.	s. d.	s. d.	s. d.
	5										
	6										
	7										
	8										
	9										
	10										
	11										
1 Foot or	12										
	13										
	14										
	15										
	16										
	17										
1½ Feet or	18										
	19										
	20										
	21										
	22										
	23										
2 Feet or	24										
	25										
	26										
	27										
	28										
	29										
	30										
	31										
	32										
	33										
	34										
	35										
3 Feet or	36										
	37										
	38										
	39										
	40										
	41										
	42										
	43										
	44										
	45										
	46										
	47										
4 Feet or	48										
3 parts or ¼ in.											
6 parts or ½ in.											
9 parts or ¾ in.											

PLATE VII.

W. Cooper, Delt. Edint.   G. Aikman, Sculpt.

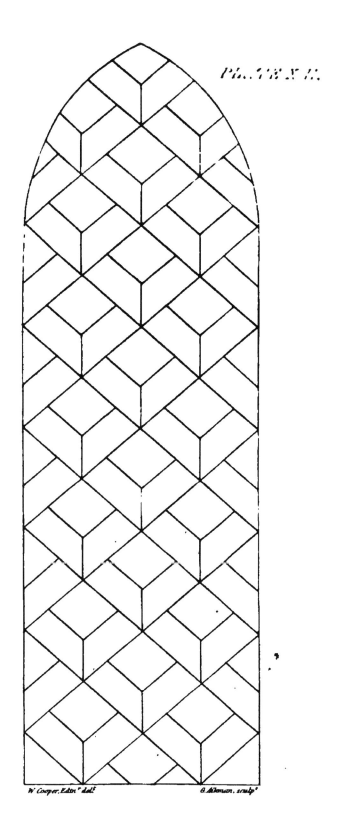

W. Cooper. Edin.ʳ del.ᵗ   G. Aikman, sculp.ᵗ

Plate V

W. Cooper. Edin.' del.'   G. Aikman. sculp.'

Fig. 1.

PLATE XV.

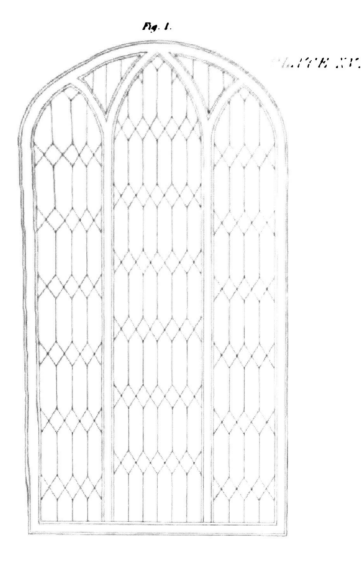

Fig. 2.

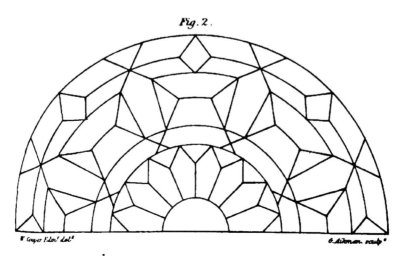

W. Cooper Edin.ᵗ del.ᵗ   G. Aikman sculp.ᵗ

PLATE XVII.

W Cooper, Delt Edin!.   G. Aikman.

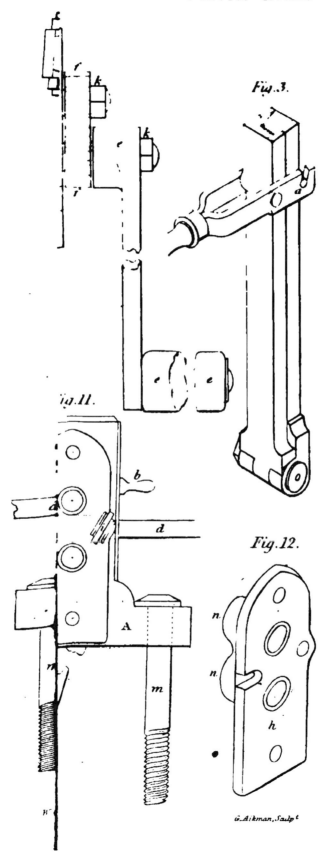

PLATE XVIII.

Fig.3.

Fig.11.

Fig.12.

G. Aikman, Sculpt

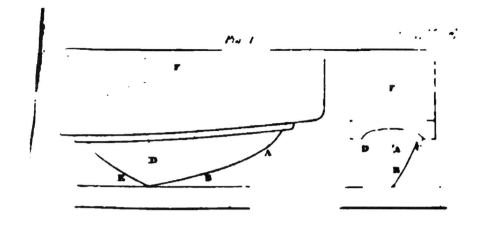

Fig. 1

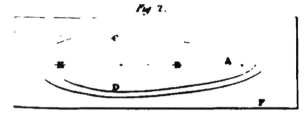

Fig. 2.

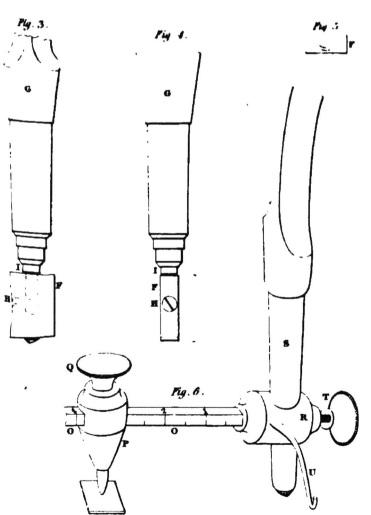

Fig. 3.

Fig. 4.

Fig. 5.

Fig. 6.

W Cooper. Edin.ᵗ delᵗ

CPSIA information can be obtained at www.ICGtesting.com
Printed in the USA
LVOW131748041211

257762LV00012B/135/P

9 781141 089758